What If... Why Not?

MOHAMED MALIKI

Copyright © 2025 by Mohamed Maliki

All rights reserved.

This book or any portion thereof may not be reproduced or used in any manner whatsoever without the express written permission of the respective author of the respective story, except for the use of brief quotations in a book review.

The writer of the respective work holds sole responsibility for the originality of the content and IndiePress is not responsible in any way whatsoever.

Printed in India

ISBN: 978-93-7197-029-7

First Printing, 2025

IndiePress

A division of Nasadiya Technologies Private Ltd.

Koramangala, Bengaluru

Karnataka-560029

http://indiepress.in/

Edited by MAP Systems, Bengaluru

Proofread by Sriya MS

Typeset by MAP Systems, Bengaluru

Book Cover designed by Sankhasubhro Nath

Publishing Consultant: Samyuktha Prasanan

Foreword

-Ratan Tata-

I found myself pleasantly surprised by the volume: *What If... Why Not?* written by my dear friend, Ambassador Maliki, as he embarks on an exciting journey in this book.

While the opening pages reflect on his diverse personal identity, as a Moroccan, a scholar of history, a traveller and a delightful companion, the kind of person everyone would want in their life, the book soon becomes a prism of thoughts reflecting the multifaceted competencies of its storyteller. Through the unravelling of the numerous incidents and experiences enumerated in the course of this reading, the volume offers a commendable starting point for an engaging conversational exchange between reader and writer, centred around the content. But to reduce this book to merely shared experiences is only half the truth and would grossly trivialise the range and depth of the writer's expertise, as evidenced in this presentation.

From the outset, the book foregrounds a somewhat offbeat approach, in that it ceases to be strictly autobiographical. At the same time, it holds a collection of singular experiences, along with a smattering of family stories, particularly from his early years, which, by and large, is a primary resource of personal anecdotes for any writer. But thereafter, by integrating an alternative choice of narration, the author has turned the conservative content of biographical writing on its head through his multiform presentation, fully substantiating the title of the volume, *What If... Why Not?*

The hallmark of this narrative is not merely the unravelling of its somewhat provocative title—which to my mind, effectively draws readers in to explore further—but coming to brass tacks, in this case, is the fact that it is threaded into this unique interface of personal stories, along with a few tales of others. The reader is also made privy to a valuable collection of life lessons that ring true across time and generations. Through the author's writing style, he manages to combine both the self and the other side, into an easy read, whereby there surfaces a harmonious mulling over of universal truths and their implications, behind the cloud of personalised surroundings.

Thus, his encounters with others are no finger-pointing episodes with a hidden agenda, nor are they mere glosses over trivial observations with a purely personal frame of reference. They are truthful and soul-searching inclusions. Nonetheless, the author has always endeavoured to move beyond the cloudiness of its immediacy and looked for the veracity of that experience in terms of its potential to yield some sprinkling of common-sense reflection.

The chapters, therefore, manage to remain within a personalised fold, yet look beyond the limits of such horizons. This distinctive style of narration, where personal anecdotage is not its central motive, nor the basis of some kind of proselytising of personal beliefs, is rare to come across in current similar accounts. The core strength of the book lies in the fact that it looks for an intrinsic genuineness that every experience carries within itself, such as the equation between the important vis-à-vis the essential, in terms of existing knowledge, thereby making it his vocabulary for enumerating interpersonal exchanges.

As a result, the book is endowed with an admirable degree of candidness. I am particularly drawn to the unique style in which he offers a glimpse into the inner workings of officialdom, through a diplomatic lens, with surprising twists and quick thinking. Rather than relying on long-winded build-ups of preliminaries or conclusions, Ambassador Maliki handpicks his choices from a basket of memorabilia. Thereafter, they are garnished with a clipped literary narration and an undercurrent of bated humour, thereby penning them into signature literary expressions. Hence, this approach of narrating the incidents becomes a precious takeaway from the volume.

Delving further into the book's highlights, is the author's ability to build strong relationships, including our own friendship, which I deeply value. The chapter dedicated to our special bond—between India and Morocco—is heart-warming. His exchanges with Indian friends, officials, and leaders, only a few of which are included in this volume, are equally exhilarating. These associations, pulsed with life, are seen here through the lens of a gifted storyteller. They not only create a strong connection with the reader, but make me believe that the book's appeal lies in its personal and relatable storytelling style, which has all the makings of a fireside chat.

I am grateful for our friendship and honoured to be part of the author's first-ever published book, conceived, written, and published in India, much to our mutual satisfaction. I will cherish this warm association forever.

Foreword

-Dr. Shashi Tharoor-

In *What if ... Why Not?*, Mohamed Maliki draws us into the exhilarating whirl of his three-decade journey across countries and cultures. Looking out of the castle of his kaleidoscopic past, he ruminates on what lessons humanity might draw from his place in the world, which, even as it swings from posting to posting across the globe, remains grounded in the mesmerising ethos of Morocco: the land he loves beyond measure. Instead of underscoring what sets these countries and cultures apart, Maliki highlights what binds us together as human beings, our numberless differences notwithstanding. Thus he emphasises the "universally common and shared values through which," over the course of his storied diplomatic career, he has forged "strong friendships with people of all kinds and across all age groups."

As he leads us from the boisterous and bustling boulevards of the Indian subcontinent to the stormy skies of Cameroon, and from the high-stakes solemnity of diplomatic negotiations to the small, intimate moments at home that matter just as much, Maliki traverses both geography and soul, much as another Moroccan traveller and explorer—Ibn Battuta—so abidingly did centuries ago.

Philosophical without being prosaic, and enlightening without being preachy, Mohamed Maliki's *What if... Why Not?* is a tender, wise, and luminous chronicle, glazed in electric wit and candour, of a life led in service not only of a nation, but of human connection.

Thanks, Gratitude, and Appreciation

To:

My beloved mother, Lalla Zineb

My lovely wife, Karima, for her unconditional support

My two princesses, Ghita and Nada

My sisters and brothers

My successive Ministers

My dear friend, the Honourable Dr Shashi Tharoor, for being so kind and generously elegant to me

My real friends and colleagues, from whom I learnt a lot and shared even more…

* * * * *

To:

Mr Harun Riaz and
Mrs Subhra Mazumdar
for believing in me.

In Memory of

I wanted to dedicate this humble work in the memory of two persons—one Moroccan and the other Indian—who left at different stages of my life. May their souls rest in peace and be accepted in Heaven. These two unique individuals not only counted a lot in my life but also had a great impact on me, my thinking, and perceptions. In fact, they represent an open teaching book full of wisdom and determination, not only for me but for many others:

- *My late father, Ssi Ahmed, as all liked to call him, was, by all means, a man ahead of his time. He taught us the value of things, not their price, and to especially deliberate over problems which can't be solved by money. Despite his death 24 years ago, I still live by many of his teachings, lessons, and wisdom.*
- *My late friend, Ratan Tata, who sadly left us in 2024, prematurely. A living legend in his time, a semi-god for many, the most caring, giving, and humble human being. The fact is that I was extremely lucky to have had him as a friend, whom he liked to address as "a true friend". Yet, I can't seem to find the accurate adjective to describe him. Nonetheless, I haven't found a better expression of gratitude than to dedicate a full chapter to our friendship. He, in*

return, graciously accepted to write the foreword of this volume, wholeheartedly.

Both the foreword and the chapter dedicated to him have been kept deliberately unchanged from the original versions, as a minimum tribute, in respect of his memory and of his authentic approval of the same.

Late Ssi Ahmed and Mr Tata have left us, but their love will remain unaltered in my heart.

Contents

Introduction	1
Why Should I Write?	5
Footprints on the Sands of Time	11
Early Age Funs And Pitfalls	20
The Budding Scholar	30
Bonding Around Food	37
Life's Best Educators	47
Path Readjustment	57
Academic Track	69
The Important and the Essential	81
Balance and Moderation	96
Bandit Capers	108
When There is a Will…	124
Deepening Diplomatic Skills	138
A Wish Becoming Reality	146
The Softer Side of Diplomacy	154

The Pride of Belonging	169
A Uniquely Built Friendship	182
What Doesn't... Makes You Stronger	200
We Have Come Thus Far	210

Introduction

As the reader goes through the engaging details of this volume, the immediate reaction might be that the contents of the entire book cannot be viewed from one single angle, or classified under one particular category.

Indeed, at the early stage of the volume, the writer attempts to take the reader along on a journey reflecting the state of mind in which he had been before writing this book. At that time, the answer to why he should or shouldn't write a book became paramount. Again, when the apprehension linked to the "what to write"—and what may be of interest to the reader—is overcome, the "how to write" becomes even more challenging for a diplomat still in service.

Soon after being in the comfort of reading parts of the writer's life including, but not limited to, his "Early Age Funs and Pitfalls" and a few events during his school years, especially in the very first chapters, we soon discover that it is not by and large a conformist autobiography. Indeed, it is about the lifestyle of the writer and the way he was brought up within a Moroccan household. All this is reflected in the set-up to understand a few critical standpoints in the persona of the writer. The events narrated in these pages, selected at random, rather than arranged chronologically, have been done for a good reason and purpose. They add to the broad understanding of the family, from social, educational and environmental angles.

The events have also been chosen for either their funny side or for the life lessons that are meant to be shared with the reader. Both elements coincide somewhere and connect somehow through the reading and sharing of experiences. Thus, each reader becomes a part of the book because, despite being driven by the strength of autobiography, the book soon becomes a philosophical perspective delving into the *why* behind the choices we make. The book depicts how we, human beings, override the *important* things over the *essential* ones in our lives, a theme to which more than a full chapter is dedicated. This concept comes up very often, through lived and illustrated experiences, and one that reared their heads, every now and then.

Since we are shaped by our environment, the writer has not hesitated to reveal a few of the traumatic experiences which have changed his life altogether and the way of his thinking. More importantly, his perception with regard to a range of behavioural conscientiousness comes to the forefront, whereby the value of things overrides the price of things. This mature conviction has guided him in his personal life and in the upbringing of his daughters. It also illustrates how he is striving to apply the same principles in his official life, while interacting with both his colleagues and the hierarchy.

On the other hand, as a diplomat still in service, the book takes you through a colourful journey to different places. These have not only enriched his experiences but have broadened his mind and understanding, particularly as a Moroccan, first and foremost. They also reflect the universally common and shared values through which he builds strong friendships with people of all kinds and across all age groups.

INTRODUCTION

All these factors remain intrinsically of great value to the writer, from which the reader can conceive how they could help them navigate more easily, through the many and somewhat similar situations he has been in, or undergone. Ultimately, from whatever angle they could be seen, it is fully left for the reader to decide. The narrated events have been life lessons for the writer, from which he emerged stronger and through which he hopes the involved reader would avoid those pitfalls that he has experienced and so generously shared.

Besides all these differing angles, the volume could be seen through a historic lens—one in which the pride of belonging is perfectly illustrated through detailed research into the history of the country he belongs to, Morocco, and which remains one of the oldest nation-states and kingdoms in the world. This country has contributed immensely to human civilisation through education, architecture, and culture, and it enjoys a phenomenal number of historical and cultural heritage sites. These elements make him connect easily with people of a country like India. This country-continent with an unparalleled civilisational heritage helps the readers recognise themselves within its unique elements. They all bestow on the narrator the specificity that couldn't be mistaken and through which any person belonging to this land of the great traveller Ibn Batuta would be not just easily, but instantly, recognised.

In sum, the book is not intended for a specific category of readers, but the writer wishes, through this book, to provide a good and pleasant read for all. Moreover, he hopes that the reading of this volume would be as rewarding and gratifying a journey as it has been for him through this modest endeavour.

Chapter 1

Why Should I Write?

In every one of us hides a writer—or at least a storyteller. Our lives are made up of different stories, be they ours or others; the ones that we would like to share, and others we would prefer to keep to ourselves. Yet, the rhetorical questions I was asking myself, before embarking on this journey, were *why* and *what should I write* or, conversely and equally intriguing, *why shouldn't I write??* The first two queries came entirely from me, while the third was from the other "me" and those who would see in me a potential writer of interest, and would naturally push for implementing this project. The fact is that the two questions remained present for a long time, and each sought supremacy over the other. The more I thought of it, the more the idea became frightening, yet fascinating, to the extent of becoming an obsession. However, stories remain personal experiences or fiction, and people share their ideas when they want and for reasons only they know. Why not me??

While the tales and experiences intermingle different cultures, people remain specific in their individual nature, as they are the product of their environment. However, the same environment doesn't necessarily produce identical human beings in their way of thinking, except for a common or universal reference they would logically share. I admit, though, that there is no logic to this statement, in so many ways. So much the better, for that is what makes the diversity, the difference, and the beauty of life itself. Thus, being able to share one's own stories remains, I believe, God's gift and a blessing in itself, as it contributes, however narrowly, to the making of history. In other words, each of us holds a small and proper narrative, which may or may not contribute to a larger understanding of our era, both in the present and in the near or far future.

But, the truth is, we have lost millions of stories that remained untold—accounts whose narration could have greatly deepened our understanding of this broad understanding. If I take my own country's story with this part of the world—India in particular—as an example, only the stories told by our ancestors in fragments have revealed how deep and far back our connections have been.

This particular story takes me back, naturally, to Ibn Battuta, who, after returning home from his travels in 1349, and at the order of the Marinid ruler of Morocco, Abu Inan Faris, dictated an account in Arabic of his travels to different parts of the globe, which covered about 44 modern-day countries, including India where he stayed for more than a decade. The Sultan of Morocco was so fascinated by his stories that he ordered Ibn Battuta to pen them down and leave them as a legacy for mankind. Though he was not a writer himself—as his book was written by Ibn Juzayy, a scholar he had previously met in Granada—he certainly was, and by all means, a good storyteller and a fine observer, with a phenomenal capacity for description, to the extent that most historians, especially the European ones, believed for centuries that he was purely and simply inventing his stories.

About the fascination that these stories offer to the reader, in his book *The Rihla* (The Travels of Ibn Battuta), without getting into the complex query if they were accurate or invented, true or false, there is a great deal of satisfaction that historians, as late as the 19th century, concluded them to be true pieces of anthropology. Its image descriptions helped them and ordinary readers to know better about India, among other lands, its peoples, customs, traditions, wares, food and so forth. As the Qazi of Islam in India, for a certain time, he was at the heart of the society and remained very close to the people, their daily lives, and problems. He had observed, and his stories taught us that there was no disharmony in society, ethnic or otherwise, and he depicted a perfect coexistence between its multiethnic peoples at that time.

The story of Abu Al Barakat Al-Barbari is another perfect example of the importance of keeping records and narrating stories, especially great stories that change the course of history. It shows how the entire archipelago of the Maldives was converted to Islam, as far back as the 12th Century, owing to this man of religion and belief, who left his country, Morocco, to spread the word of God armed only with his faith and the Holy Quran. The stream of history, a story told by Ibn Battuta himself, is about the man who changed the history of the Maldivian people forever. The result is that the Maldivians have been strongly, and still are, emotionally linked to Morocco. The Day of their Conversion is annually celebrated to date. I wonder how we would have apprehended this big moment in the history of the Maldives if it had not been told by persons like Ibn Battuta. Likewise, a good number of the Muslims in Sri Lanka claim, according to the same author, to be of Moroccan origin.

If I am asked why I brought up this part of our common history, through the lenses of Ibn Battuta, and his links with many countries in this part of the world, especially India, the Maldives and Sri Lanka, I would say it's my own way of paying a special tribute to this Great Man, but even more, in expressing frustration at all the other stories which were not told. Indeed, I am pretty sure that many others preceded him, or came after him, who might have had similar experiences, if not better ones, and whose stories were never told, and to our regret, are lost forever. Since stories become history, many of them may give a meaning to our present, but also would provide answers to our raised questions and interrogations to better understand our own past and, probably equally important, to better appreciate our present.

In that sense, we will always remain indebted to the Sultan of Morocco, who foresaw and valued the importance of immortalising those moments the Great Traveller had lived, describing the lives of different peoples and cultures through his keen lens. The efforts he put in and the positions he was able to hold in the various countries he had crossed or lived in, reflected also the grandeur of the empire he belonged to, Morocco. Indeed, he was giving as much of his own culture as he was receiving from others.

By all means, I feel a special pride in considering Ibn Battuta to be a very distinguished Envoy since he was charged by the then ruler of India, Muhammad bin Tughlaq, who was renowned as one of the most powerful men in the Muslim world at that time, to undertake a very sensitive diplomatic mission to the Emperor of China.

However, I don't pretend, in the least, that telling a few of my stories and views could be of the same value or interest; nor do I wish this ongoing project to have this wide international impact. Yet, my hope is that my modest attempt to share bits of my experiences and a few stories that impose themselves on me or have come naturally, will serve and help others avoid or learn from the mistakes, pitfalls or misjudgments I have made in my life. It is also my way of sharing what I believe were learning moments, at least in my understanding, and the things that I wouldn't have done, if I had to go through the same experiences again.

WHY SHOULD I WRITE?

But do I regret it? Of course not. The choices we make and the decisions we take are what make the beauty of life, because you learn from your and others' experiences, and even much more from one's pitfalls. Didn't we learn in school and from books that he who ignores history is condemned to repeat it?! Isn't it true that no one can guess what could transpire in the next few minutes or hours of life? Doesn't the path the *divine* has laid out for each one of us remain invisible to the human eye? Aren't the winds of change that blow past us, though turbulent at times, and the force that often guides us, all lead towards the direction which is predestined for us?

As a man of faith, I am strongly of the thought that regardless of how strange or chaotic the changes of our life may be, I believe everything happens in its own time, in its due course, with a reason, and certainly for a purpose. Conceiving to write this book in the middle of the COVID-19 Pandemic, obeys indeed, the same order, and that everything comes in its own due time!! Ultimately, just as much as it is about sharing my stories within a story, and as I was putting order in my thoughts, without yet putting them down, it dawned on me just how much I would be, not only receiving from this experience but also rediscovering myself.

In fact, in the course of this journey, I have been going through a process of reading and reassessing my own past through the lenses of my current perspective. All the events that characterised my life, the decisions I took, or those I couldn't, for a good reason at that time, and those that shaped my future, I have come to perceive them in a different manner.

I had certainly, without meaning it, shaped my future at that time, which may be my present now, only to end up understanding it under a different light, and it is already gratifying. So I presume that the coming fragmented stories imposed on me for a certain reason, or without, are all a journey within a journey, a quest that has been in itself a rewarding experience, an experience which I hope will be as much of an interest to you, my dear reader, as it has been so far, for this small human being that I am.

Chapter 2

Footprints on the Sands of Time

It is often a little bewildering when one actually begins to conceive of penning down a book about oneself. My case was no exception. It is generally known that in life, we keep things personal for ourselves. These may be struggles. These may comprise very good or even funny moments. They do not necessarily add something to the life of a person, but they could be "small windows". I would say these moments were often, if not mostly, like a nice breeze that comes into one's life. Yet, it could be moments clouded with troubles. It could be a person you meet by chance. It could be a book that triggers deep and almost forgotten memories, refreshed once again.

Thus, like others of my ilk, I too must have gone through all the above phases. The fact is I actually never thought of having enough energy or even reasons to write, especially being a diplomat still in service.

But once I was cornered into doing it, the idea began to overwhelm, if not haunt me.

Initially, when such thoughts filled me, there was high elation at the prospect of actually putting those memorable moments on paper—portraying, in a sense, the journey of my life. Then came phases of sober reflection on the prudence of such a venture, which sometimes gave way to sinking to the depths of depression about not matching up to the task I was undertaking. It brought on bouts of unexplained fright at the task I was planning, and the entanglement it might bring.

Ultimately, the answer became evident when I realised that commitment to this exercise was going to be a kind of challenge. Within days of my decision, I was faced with the usual barrage of misgivings. The nagging oppression during this period, which beset my waking hours in fleeting escapades, concerned the kind of approach I should adopt in carrying out the responsibility of showcasing myself as a writer. Like any other professional, positioned at the helm of affairs at the time of this writing, I had a plethora of choices before me. But through all these possibilities, there flowed the inevitability of a Hobson's choice syndrome, as they came with their own set of complexities. My train of thought led me to analyse this book project by a process of thinking through, or self-examination.

If I had to go back to that time, I thought, by recalling events in my life in hindsight, I would not do things a certain way. This, I felt, was an advantage because I would profit from the absence of any background morality that had dogged my mind at the time of the incident. But at the same time, over the span of years, I could still feel connected with them, and because I am different from the person I was then, a review of the past happenings, I realised, is not necessarily a revival of them. The events I would record in the course of my writing made me introspect about why they had come to my recall at that time. After all, I didn't consciously look for them… those persons, books, "windows" in my life, they came back by themselves.

And sometimes, it becomes clear that you need only one thing to put all thoughts in place; everyday concerns, philosophical questions, and more. Hence, we should apply historical wisdom to our personal lives as well. The many generations who have lived before us must have gone through experiences much like ours. They, too, if given a chance, I felt, would have been quite happy to share their experiences with others. So, this train of thought led me to see the other person who would appear in my personal anecdotes as one who is involved like me, engaged with my book.

This feeling of a shared venture made me reflect on yet another trait in my persona. All through my life, I have never wanted to exploit the weaknesses of others. Even if I have to fight with somebody, since childhood, I felt I should make sure that they are fit and ready. This trait reflects even when we play a game now and then, be it billiards (snooker) or table tennis, to enjoy and unwind from work. I have always wanted my challenger to be an equal. I prefer to compete on a level playing field.

Somehow, this mindset makes it a little more comfortable for the other person to engage with me. Even during COVID times, despite the difficult situation we were all facing, I convinced my colleagues not to hesitate in offering assistance to any Moroccan stranded in the five countries we cover, however strange the request may have been. Hypothetically, if somebody were to ask, 'I need a razor for my beard', I would say: 'Okay, we will try to accommodate your needs'. I don't necessarily have "no" in mind. I always say: 'Yes, let me see if it can be done'. Thus, from the very beginning, I try to give as much positivity as possible to that person; something I hope my colleagues, friends, and of course my family members would adopt and share.

Having established what role other people would play in this journey, my initial dilemma remained unresolved. Should the book be a kaleidoscope of my lived experiences only? Should it contain a commentary alongside my feelings and the outcomes of my actions as related in the incident? Should it highlight the lessons learned? But in that case, not every case had future consequences. Also, a subsequent sobering effect gripped my thinking as this mental debate began to gain ground. Hence, I recoiled to the question of whether it was worth the effort of writing a book of this kind. All these random reactions led to the feeling of chasing my own tail, as my deliberations led nowhere. It only brought me back to square one.

Yet, even in the darkest of moments along this penning of my personal journey, and despite spasms of despondent moods, I realised that though something held me back from writing the volume, there was never a question of abandoning the project altogether. In fact, the pull in this direction supplanted all other considerations. Fortunately, this feeling of finding the courage to write my memoir began to gain ground with the passage of time and triggered a new sense of excitement. Before long, it led me to reflect on why I considered myself the right candidate to write the story of my life from a personal perspective, rather than delegating this task to a biographer. I decided to examine this further.

Back at the proverbial drawing board once again, another practical difficulty came to the surface. I had never written down any notes for a memoir. I was not in the habit of regularly jotting down details. Also, I had lost sight of the only diaries I had ever had, in which I had jotted down, irregularly, happenings off and on. Maybe I lost them while serving in Cameroon. But then my inner voice—so to speak—beckoned. Was I not the person who liked to live in the mode of the "today"? The person who does not repeat things? Hence, the angles by which I would tackle this "autobiography" would not be a copy-paste job of yesterday's memories written from an old diary entry. If I compare past events to the present, it would be a simple rehash of memories, and as a writer, I would lapse into repetition, rehashing those instances as they had occurred then.

How reassured I felt by this explanation! It meant that for writing my book, I would rely on happenings that came back to my mind. It would be as if the thing lying in the depths suddenly jumped to view and, thereafter, I began to remember things which my mind allowed access to or, in truth, I wished to remember; an exercise to explore my past. Of course, at this point, an external "push" loomed in the form of my friend, Haroon Riaz, who had always seen in me a literary critic and, at the same time, a storyteller. This became even more conspicuous for him while bringing out, together, the Embassy's yearly Magazine, *Morocco in Focus*, of which he was the editor. He always urged me, for many years, to pen my memoirs and share my thoughts, which he found interesting, with a wider readership. I would say he ended up getting what he wanted, and I will always remain grateful to him for pushing hard to spark my curiosity to take this idea forward.

So, as a starting premise, it struck me that my profession as a career diplomat had equipped me with the right mindset—at least so I was made to believe—along with the requisite tools to pen my own story in a manner that would be an interesting read for others. After all, I had not just travelled to several places and met a cross-section of humanity, per se, or ticked off places I had visited in the manner of an indefatigable—but certainly a modest—globetrotter. Through my professional training, I had also developed a liking for learning about my surroundings with an above average accuracy and, more importantly, genuine interest. This acquired ability has given me a wide-angled view on life, as it has exposed me to a variety of situations and geared me to nurture my ability in these circumstances to write my ideas in quality prose, so as to leave a mark on readers' minds.

An added confidence surged through me when I assessed my ability to skilfully engage with my listener or reader. Incidentally, my Ministers and senior fellows used to find me "a good listener". I realised that with this ability I was already taking baby steps towards a meaningful engagement with the reader, to whom I intended to narrate, not only parts of my life's journey but my way of thinking and my philosophy of life as well.

Further analysis of my inherent advantages for this task made clear to me that my profession had coached me into developing a fondness for observing details, however trivial they might appear, which I presume would help me to focus on minor personal anecdotage so as to "colour" my writing with the right amount of pep. Of course, the icing on the cake was almost like a conjurer's trick. In the practice of my profession over these years, I have realised that I must take the lead position in setting an agenda for myself, which, in case of an autobiographical exercise, entailed choosing or eliminating what I deemed fit, or unfit, for my purpose.

Thus, the task of writing, which I intended to pursue, would be characterised with a degree of self-editing throughout. This would make it come forth, even in its embryonic juncture, as a work that is penned with the dual advantages of methodical writing and simultaneous self-editing, during the course of its creation.

Sidestepping from the main course, at this juncture, a tempting alternative presented itself: I began toying with the idea of structuring the work according to my tenures in various parts of the world, as also in Morocco itself. This idea lingered tantalisingly for some time. For one, I would stand out through my year-on-year narration of my experiences, and even more importantly, this would also shipshape my writing into a formulated elegance.

But alas! This train of thought, too, was short-lived, as it soon soured when I realised that such an approach would turn the concept of an autobiography on its head and splice it into a mere memoir, albeit of considerable length. I was left heaving and taking in deep breaths of Yogic contemplation. I gazed out of my office window in New Delhi until I was distracted by the roar of an aeroplane flying over the area towards its final destination, a few miles away from the Indira Gandhi International Airport.

When the idea had been left to gnaw at my sensibilities for some days, the folly of this move dawned on me. As I have chosen to pen this memoir at a time when I am serving as my country's representative not just to India, but also as the Ambassador to the Kingdom of Bhutan, the Republic of Maldives, the Democratic Socialist Republic of Sri Lanka, and to Nepal, my official commitments entail extensive travel as well as other responsibilities that take a toll of endless work hours each day. Thus, I am often obliged to continue at my work desk beyond the scheduled hours.

These unique circumstances often mean stretching my workday two to three hours beyond the official closing time at the Embassy. Together with me, my colleagues have cheerfully borne the burden of staying back into the late evening to ensure that the work is completed on time and is not put off until the next day. It so happens that a glass of freshly brewed mint tea, prepared earlier, is replenished every now and then to keep my senses refreshed, in the absence of my regular espresso coffee. Of course, I try to ensure, as much as I can, that the same individuals are not made to suffer my unearthly work routine because I try to rotate duties at the office, making it a sharing and caring round-up schedule.

The singular entity without an available substitute to take his place beyond office hours is the driver of the official car. In his case, I try to compensate for the "torture" I inflict on him by offering, occasionally, to drive home myself when there is no official meeting or duty in the city. All this self-confession, dear reader, is to apprise you of the impracticalities of a country-cum-tenure-centric approach to my writing scheme.

The one good outcome of this round of self-examination has been that I have now been able to mentally chalk out what this writing exercise should eliminate. I realised that it should not be country-centric content, nor should it be confined to any particular category of readership. I wanted my effort to be shared with as wide a group as possible, including times when I would be able to offer it to friends and family members. Hence, it could not take on the garb of my official journey alone.

Thus, the proverbial gavel was dropped on the decision to set about writing this book as a free-flowing thought process where the events would be narrated in their natural appearance in my consciousness, without being severely partitioned into artificial slots, or demarcations of time and place. It would not be a logical drawing up of genealogical references from family sources either, as that would section my labours into rigid formality, stripping away the frolicsome and distinctive character of a personal history.

On this note, I therefore let the matter rest for a while before taking up the project for a second time. This time, much like a confident pupil who has managed to complete all his homework submissions prior to arriving at school on a particular day, I am a more self-assured undertaker of this task. Yes, this book was intended to be a personal journey to be shared with my reader, but the incidents and landmarks in it were to be chosen in an astute manner. Instead of just a recounting of experiences in a calendar format or any other strictures, the choice of narratives worthy of inclusion would be based on the imprints they had left in my mind over the years.

This approach would rescue the book from falling prey to a mere stringing together of anecdotes, as I have decided to include those incidents that have left a lingering residue only and not a gamut of disconnected happenings. With such a course of action, only those incidents and lifestyle inclusions would see themselves in print on the pages that were worthwhile as life lessons.

This handful of indelible memories that I would narrate across the pages of my personal effort would carry with them the potential of life-changing instrumentalities. They would be incidents in my life which have the making of "footprints on the sands of time"... a time which was an important milestone in the shaping of my life, both abroad and at home, in Morocco. This unique land that has given me enough reasons to admire, and whose rich history has definitely determined the shaping of my life and who I am. I will always be imbued with the foremost feeling that I could never give back what I have received or taken from my beloved country.

Chapter 3

Early Age Funs and Pitfalls

Of my earliest personal memories in my large and happy household, is one linked to the way I was addressed by everyone. Instead of calling me by my name, Mohamed, my friends and young uncles used to call me "Mani Lalmani", meaning "Mohamed, The German", where "Mani" was used in a pleasant way for a child named "Mohamed". Looking back, I found it an aberration for the name of no other than the Prophet, Peace Be Upon Him. Then, "Lalmani" means "The German" in Arabic, both spoken and written. This was because I had partly yellowish hair as a child, though one would hardly link my later black hair and the present state of greying to that category anymore.

Besides this comic reference linked to my childhood, another memory that has stayed with me is about the day I had my circumcision, a ritual of paramount importance in Islam. Unlike the present times in Morocco, and in most of the Islamic countries, where it is performed in hospitals generally, this ceremony was always done in our homes and open for all family members, friends, and neighbours.

What I most remember of the day is the way I was given all the attention possible by everyone in the family. Along with me, there was also my younger brother, who at that time was a baby, not exceeding seven days of his life. Naturally, the quota of attention given to him would hardly have matched mine on that day and in fact it didn't, and it wouldn't have made any difference for him. Indeed, what was taking place hardly mattered to a newborn blissfully unaware of his surroundings. The majority viewpoint about the best time for this ceremony was that it should be performed as early as possible in one's life so that there's no trauma. But all these logical deliberations were not my concern. On that day, all that mattered was being the centre of attention and attraction, with everyone being so nice and agreeable to me. Visitors and guests with gifts were constantly streaming in and they made it a point to spend some time with me. The predominant memory is that I was beside myself with happiness. There were sweets galore making the rounds and, of course, dry fruits in plenty and anything that I asked for was being magically brought and given to me. I didn't know the counter price of all this.

Eventually, the household barber arrived, who was accompanied by my father and a few of his friends. The whole episode took place on the rooftop of the house. There were people all around. What I remember from that time is the actual moment. After the stage of the operation was set up, so to speak, the barber, with his scissors in hand, tried to distract me by diverting my attention elsewhere. When everything was ready and everybody was fixated on me, like in a dramatic irony, he suddenly said: 'Oh look! There's a nice bird flying in the sky'. Thus, I didn't see what he was doing as my eyes had wandered skywards in search of that "nice bird". Hence, if you ask me if I remember the episode as painful, I will certainly say 'no'. Over time, circumcision has been approved medically for its health benefits, too. Even urine, mainly at a young age, was acknowledged to be an antiseptic.

As for my baby brother, it was also his *Akika* day—baptism ceremony. He was given the name of Abdelali on that day as well. And part of this feting and pampering was also carried out in the way of traditional wear too. The dress that I was given on that day, the *kachaba*, was a green one with some silver or goldish designs on it, besides white *babouche* slippers. Whatever it was, the dress, which was usually worn by anyone in my situation on this once in a lifetime occasion, added to my feeling of being special and the cynosure of all eyes. With the family all around, the environment that was created was magical and took away the suffering it entailed. I was a small king on that day—and though my brother was sharing the importance too, he was too young to grasp the situation.

Among all present, no one could dismiss the apprehension appearing on the faces of both my father and mother. However, the fear did not appear as visible on my father's face as it was on my mother's, for he managed to hide it, while in fact those who knew him more closely could see that anxiety was there. After all, circumcision may have some risks as well. Fortunately, the fright my mother had shown at the beginning soon vanished as, all had gone well, giving way to joy and amusement. The long ululations she gave, replicated by all the women around, marked the start of the day-long ceremony. I recall she was superbly dressed, and I can remember her hair, perfectly plaited on either side, was swaying to the rhythm and reflected the atmosphere of joy. My father and the other gentlemen guests had left after taking a cup of tea and snacks, served immediately after the ceremony was over, but only to return later for the feast.

There was dancing happening all around that day. There were so many lady visitors. All the shyness among the women disappeared once the men had left. They formed groups, with some playing drums and others singing altogether. Then the ladies spontaneously exchanged roles between playing drums, singing and dancing, and though the attention was still on me, the audience profited from this instance. I recall in particular my two uncles, Abdellah and Mohamed, who were also living at home with us. I think they had the most fun on that day, along with my aunt, Aziza, who was only forty days older than me, because they remained the most prominent people around me from that memory, due to the narrow age gap between us. While the dancing and singing were going on, they stuck to me all the time and relished the largesse of the sweets I had received, which they enjoyed more than I did! I still have a mental image of the day as if it had happened only yesterday!

In later years, I have sometimes been asked why the whole procedure was not done in a hospital, as is prevalent now. I feel that if I had been admitted to a hospital, it would have robbed all the fun and amusement of the occasion. It would certainly have been a trauma for a four-year-old, because even at that age, going to a hospital, especially for a child, is itself a moment of tension and anxiety. You immediately associate the place with something being or going wrong. As a family occasion, it became sans trauma and definitely a unifying force, a moment of joy and happiness for all the family and friends, like all the instances of privilege in our life that we always cherish and value.

As is my habit, every incident that has a recall element in later years for me leaves behind a trailblazer of high points on my learning curve. This event was no exception. When trying to reason out why a home-based occasion was the better option, I am tempted to put forth the phenomenon of a glass half filled with water. While the positivist examines it as half full, the negativist looks upon it as half empty. On my part, I have looked at it with positivity because it is the oldest happy memory I can remember, and that makes it special. Also, it was a memory where the human had triumphed over the pragmatic, and it certainly left its residue of togetherness and oodles of joy for a four-year-old, on his special day of initiation into another beginning, yet unknown to me as a boy.

To my mind, this incident was the most lucid memory of my childhood. Maybe it was so because it was the first and earliest happy family gathering I attended, and even more so, because it was organised in my honour. I am sure there were many more before. The previous one, I would guess, was the birth of my sister, Aicha, who is two years younger than me, yet, I do not have a single hint of that event.

I also recall that special day for quite another reason. As is customary, we had received a lot of sugar packets as presents. Sugar was the most popular gift exchanged between families on almost all occasions, both happy and sad. These were 'dressed' into solid blocks of approximately two kg weight, each, and wrapped in violet coloured paper, as if it were a toy. As the guest count on the occasion was large, the sugar packets were proportionately substantial in number, and soon they filled up a great portion of an entire medium-sized room. I recall a post-event conversation about selling off this huge sugary hoard, as it was not only the common custom, but also it seemed the most logical option, as there were too many to keep for home consumption only. I had piped up on hearing about the sale proposition, saying, 'No... I can't allow you. Let us keep all this sugar. It will come in handy at my wedding. So, keep them till my marriage day,' I had pleaded, in a serious and rising tone while showing I was concerned and arguing, like a man insisting his voice be heard too, much to the amusement of everyone around.

But that rationale from a four-year-old was not only humorous. It was couched in more than just plain problem-solving. Though for many, I was an innocent boy, the remark was an eye-opener to an element of foresight displayed by its speaker, which I think has been a trait with me all along. The sense of farsightedness, as well as a sense of thrift and, of course, making the best use of what is available for future consumption or benefice, were all life lessons that were revealed through that logic of the sugar episode.

The building blocks of memories have other high points all through childhood. One of them is linked with my grandfather's visit to Mecca for pilgrimage, a wish that every Muslim longs to fulfil, at least once in a lifetime.

'What do you want me to bring for you from Mecca, Mohamed?' he asked me. I think it was the early seventies, and a time when wristwatches with flashy dial faces ranked high in my estimation of coveted possessions I wished to own. In particular, dial faces with luminous green or blue or even red colours were considered sophisticated taste and fashionable by my standards. Thus, when I was given a choice by my late grandfather, I had blurted out the obvious, without regard to the impropriety of such a request from a prospective "Al-Haj" by a child of no more than eight years. But grandfather had played along and promised, to my satisfaction, to return from the pilgrimage, watch in hand. The time waiting for his return was endless for a child. It was also the first gift I would receive of my own choice. It was big.

Alas! There was disappointment ahead for me, because there was no sight of a watch being visible, after gifts were distributed, as was the custom. Unable to control myself, I finally popped the question to him. Grandfather was literally shamefaced at having failed to keep his word. It had simply escaped his mind. I knew he was sincere, but it didn't help and my shock and disillusionment were so clearly visible that he ordered my father, at once in a commanding voice, to go to the souk, to Abdullah, a family friend and the only owner of the workshop for repairing and selling watches, close to us in town. 'Ahmad, bring him the watch I promised him, today, not tomorrow,' he had urged. The order was good enough to solve my problem and give me intense relief, as I knew my father could not argue and had never declined a request from his parents, since he always took their wishes for orders.

The watch soon began to rule my life. I would make it a point to tune in to the radio news bulletins at eight o'clock in the morning and evening, and at one in the afternoon. I would check against the radio for the correct time, not tolerating even one single minute before or over time. Never had anyone given such hard times to poor Abdullah, particularly as he would have done the "repairs", free of charge. In fact, I didn't care if my father had to pay for my excessive and repeated visits, without his preliminary authorisation. I was more concerned with tuning the watch's mechanism to fulfil my wish; nothing else. Abdullah was desperate in trying to convince me that nothing was wrong. I was simply a hopeless case for him. I am sure he ended up pretending, in most cases, to repair it.

I remember once that the watch had stopped working and, in my desperation, I had placed it between two pages of the Holy Qur'an. It was my way of imploring God, with a silent and unsaid longing for a near miracle. Thrilled to the extent you cannot imagine, when I checked the watch anxiously early the next day and discovered that it had started clicking! Needless to say, with my little mind and limited scope of understanding, the Qur'an became, after this happy outcome, much more than just a source of spiritual learning or a religious book for me. I learnt later that it had restarted working accidentally or incidentally, but I was not prepared to hear a rational explanation then. I somehow believed firmly that the Holy Qur'an could make miracles.

Besides the elation of possessing a watch of my own and my fascination with time, the watch episode had also shown me a side of my father's personality and his dedication to timeliness in all things. If we stayed out and did not inform him, as I had once taken the liberty of doing, the outcome was not a physical outburst. Father had uttered some profound words. 'Don't take me for granted,' he had said. 'Kindness shown is a choice I have made. Don't push me to show the other face.' The words had opened my eyes to self-realisation, in the most telling of ways, and have stayed on as just one more life lesson that I will cherish for the rest of my days.

The obsession with functional things and machines, mainly watches, stayed with me forever. Whenever my watch stopped working, especially after we had left Rissani where poor Abdullah had his shop, I would sneak into one of the less-used washrooms at home, with a knife or screw driver, open the "victim" watch and try, with self-confidence, to fix it. In most cases, the watches would become useless and be lost forever. After sending a good number of watches literally to the cemetery, my brothers and sisters were always arguing with my father not to offer me any new, or even used ones, as they knew beforehand what would soon be its destiny. This fascination has stayed with me till now. I would always try to repair things at home, including machines, before asking specialists to step in and fix them after I had failed.

But there are other light-hearted moments linked to my childhood love for things mechanical. This time round, it was my bicycle. I was a proud possessor of this gadget that propelled me from place "A" to place "B" in no time. Hence, it had to look special too. I therefore adopted a lifestyle of extreme control so that every penny was economised to buy something more to decorate my beloved cycle. Sometimes it was a bell; at other times it was an attachment such as a basket, or a fancy pillion seat, and so on. I recall I had fixed special lights and an alarm bell, too. The pedals were fitted with mirrors when the bicycle was in its heyday.

Visits to and by relatives often resulted in my being given a small cash amount, especially on Eid occasions, as a parting gift, and that money was promptly spent on yet another showpiece for my beloved bike. Thus, when I had visited my maternal grandfather, a merchant, he had dipped into his youngest son's pocket, Uncle Khlafa, and given me all the change it contained, which I now recall amounted to a sum of around ten dollars, a big amount by all standards at that time. I am sure he was not aware how much it was. That entire hoard was recklessly dedicated to a round of upgrading my cycle to greater heights of comfort and style. Still, there were always more gadgets to add to make it look unique in its kind. And the habit had grown till I was tempted, one day, to "dip" slyly into my father's pocket and extricate 20 Dirhams and put it to good use, or so reasoned the child that I was, without measuring the consequences or the gravity of my "robbery act", thinking it would go unnoticed.

Alas, the theft did not go undetected, as I had wished, and when I returned after a ride, making my way through the outer offices of the house, where father and the other officials would often sit after work, enjoying the afternoon tea and exchanging pleasantries, he casually enquired: 'Mohamed, your bicycle is becoming almost a race car, especially if you cover the seat and put on the helmet. Where did you get all this money?' he added in a very serious and authoritative manner. I lied blatantly, but deep down I was hoping I had managed to fool him because he did seem convinced, I thought, and he continued his conversation with his colleagues. Yet, I felt much discomfort throughout the evening. My fears proved right soon after.

Imagine my plight when he sent for me, while he was in the office the next day. Once there, his paramilitary guard ushered me in. He ordered and pre-warned the guard at once: 'Do not come between me and my son.' The iron ruler was held firmly as he ordered: 'Hold out the right hand... the hand with which you stole the money,' and the sharp crack of the iron ruler stung with pain even as my mind writhed in remorse for having betrayed the trust of my father. What followed thereafter cut me to the quick. 'I have given up, and you are no longer my son,' he announced. 'I don't have children who steal and lie.'

The next five or six days were a living hell on Earth, yearning for a call, a word, or a smile from him. None ever came, to my discomfort, in the whole household. Then after a week, I gathered up courage enough, as advised by my mother, who was also uncomfortable about this episode taking more time and magnitude than necessary and creating an unhappy atmosphere. After a lot of hesitation and saliva-swallowing, in and out, I ventured and said, 'Brother, (that's how I used to call my father, following my uncles' way of addressing him), I didn't take the money to use it badly.' I blabbered and begged for forgiveness. He, too, was sobered as he explained. 'Even if you wanted the money, it does not prevent you from asking for it. It is not your money. It was mine, and it was in my pocket. How can I trust you anymore? If I sit by the way and pick up something which is not mine (he remarked by way of an analogy), it is a serious sin. Neither God nor a human would forgive you for this.' That episode was soon over, but it was a life lesson to me, and by extension to everybody.

Today, I am grateful to him for setting the limits to which I could go. It was a way by which I learnt to appreciate the price of things... even more, the value of things and the limits I must place upon myself. This would avoid my falling into the pitfall of overindulgence, even though they may be trivialities, in the understanding of a boy on the brink of his teenage life.

Chapter 4

The Budding Scholar

The general consensus of opinion about the first day at school for most children is one of utter bewilderment, to put it mildly. I recall how one person described his feelings about the first day as being on another planet, where everything was strange, where everything appeared larger than life, and where one was worried about losing their way. One of them even recounted that the entrance door to the classroom, which she had set as a mental landmark of her surroundings, appeared to loom larger than a compound gate, and she wondered if she would ever be able to exit it and escape to safety!

The first day remains a landmark in a new life, more orderly and certainly constraining, both in terms of time and behaviour. But in my case, the first day was without any accompanying trauma, primarily because I had been attending the Quranic School much earlier, before being admitted to the government school. I went to school at the age of five and was happy to go along with my two uncles and aunt. So I was not necessarily concerned about having to go to school as if I was a complete stranger, or without any protection. You would hear many children crying after their parents or elders had left them to face alone their new, and often hostile, environment and destiny.

There is also an important factor behind my comfort in going to school. I believed that if I had survived the endurance of my Quranic school teacher Abduullah, the *"Fqih"*, any other teacher, in any other school, would be "fun". He would receive us in his small, dark school room before dawn, right after morning prayers, or after Maghreb prayer. Another smaller room was adjoining the bigger one, which could be accessed only by crossing the first one. It was even darker, but this didn't make any difference to the *Fqih* because he was completely blind. Then, to be able to control all the small boys and even the few attending girls, he would make sure he had a long stick by his side, long enough to reach the farthest corner of that room. Any misbehaviour or trouble caused by anyone would result in collective punishment, as the flexible stick would be moved quickly and firmly from far left to the extreme right side of the room, and vice versa, not sparing a single small soul, whose unique reason of presence was mostly to "please" the parents who insisted on our learning how to read, write, and learn by heart as many verses as possible of the Holy Qu'ran, preferably before reaching the school age. I can not dismiss the fact that he was softer when somebody would bring something from home to offer him, and of whatever nature it was (money, eggs, chicken, sugar, tea, vegetables and so on). With our little minds, we would organise secretly how to distribute the gifts to offer on different days so that he would be happy, less aggressive, and wouldn't use the cursed stick consequently.

At times, it worked, but it very often didn't, as our parents wouldn't follow our "recommendations" or logic, much to our despair. For them, that was the way it should be, and no complaint would be accepted. We also learned that it was useless and hopeless to voice any grievance, as nobody would give us a reason. The parents' behaviour gave greater freedom to the *Fqih* to impose his *diktat* and manner of education. So, when there was a long gap of no offering, most of the children would spend a scary hour, losing focus on studies, wondering when the stick would do the only job it was brought for. Consequently, going to regular school was very much of a rescue from all the trouble we used to face daily and, above all, it meant escaping from a very early wake-up, in almost an inhumane hour, for a child of less than five or six, especially during freezing or rainy winter mornings.

On the other hand, the regular routine of lessons and classroom activities were, somehow, indistinct. I imbibed lessons, I think, quite unconsciously, because the school, both the Quranic and the regular one, were becoming a normal exercise I would willingly, and sometimes even mechanically, do. This easiness came from the fact that school was within the neighbourhood and part of the geography of Rissani, where I spent my early years, till the age of ten. It was a mixed education of different subjects, including religious studies, within the same set-up. Incidentally, education was given to all children, and my school had a co-educational set-up as there were no bars to such a system, mainly during the early learning years.

But yes, I must confess right at the outset that it was not just scholarly attractions that made me excited to go to school each day. The excitement also came from the prospect of companionship and the sharing of food together, at times. School hours were from 8.30 a.m. to noon, and there was a long lunch break. School would again resume at 2:00 p.m. and continue till 5 o'clock, when it was time to go back home. The long interval of two hours at lunchtime made it possible for us to come home for lunch. We would all walk for less than fifteen minutes to reach home for a hot meal and then go back.

Besides, it was not a customary practice in Morocco of the seventies to propagate a culture of dining outside the home, as a recreational ritual. In fact, having meals at cafés or restaurants was resorted to by strangers and visitors when their other options were barred. Thus, it was generally a practice among bachelors or single people to take up this alternative. Mealtimes were exclusive home activities, and inviting guests to share food was considered to be *de rigueur*, rather than the exception. Being home at midday on a routine basis for lunch was customary.

But there were also the odd times when we schoolboys resorted to the alternative choice of having lunch, on specific days, which had been prepared at the school canteen. I cannot vouch for the gourmet calibre of this meal, but what I can remember is the cosiness of holding a warm, just-out-of-the-oven loaf, which resembled the French baguette. It was different from the usual round breads that were made at home, but what tickles my memory after this lapse of time is the toasty warmth of those loaves. They would be crisp on the outside, and as we tore them apart, the snow-white innards would be a moist white morsel as it touched our tongues. We loved to be served the things we didn't have the habit of eating at home, especially the lentils or white beans, accompanied by meat, but not always. The joy of filling either side of the long baguette with that soupy goodness was a sensation that still sends my taste buds tingling.

I can also relive the warmth and fellow feeling that those school lunches gave me, my younger uncle, and all the pupils there. We would sit together at a spot behind our classrooms after going up to the food counter to collect our share. And I can vouch for the fact that the food definitely gave me more energy when in that shared company atmosphere. In hindsight, I recall that all of us had imbibed a respect for food through this shared experience. I do not recall anyone throwing away food or wasting it.

This system of school meals was introduced primarily for children who lived at a distance from the school and could not go back for the midday meal. They were those who would cycle from early morning to reach on time. But its lasting fallout was that we also appreciated the value of communal eating and its unspoken rule of not wasting a morsel. We would generously give our food away, instead of casting it aside or throwing it away, so the midday meal was not just a way to allay the hunger pangs but also a manner of learning to respect food and the value of communion around food.

Another memory around the homely custom of sharing and serving food once took on an amusing turn, at our place. The incident goes back to the era of early electrification outreach in the countryside. Domestic supply of electricity was mostly used during the evening hours, from sunset to 11.30 p.m., and the living room of the house was the spot where this supply was fully utilised. Not only was the place fitted with electric bulbs, it also lodged the— still considered a luxury then— black-and-white TV set, which our family owned, along with very few lucky households at that time. By logic, therefore, the living room, during the scheduled telecasting hours, played a dual-purpose role. On the one hand, it was the demarcated space to share meals and complete school assignments for all of us, while on the other, it served as a gathering ground for avid TV enthusiasts and curious visitors from the neighbourhood.

In the decades of nascent electrification, television broadcasts, too, were in their black-and-white avatar. The lion's share of the content that was aired in the late sixties and early seventies, was news-related, with the telecaster rattling off the happening highlights from the studio confines, while the on-the-ground footage was edited as best as possible through the camera shots that were peppered with cartoons, Hollywood and Arabic, mostly Egyptian and Lebanese, movies, etc. What viewers usually saw was the face of a well-dressed news presenter, narrating from a written script, and with the right intonation.

For the excited viewing audience on the sitting-room floor, where the TV had a central place, the scene was no less sophisticated than the setting of an elite salon, playing host to the community. That the viewing audience arrived uninvited was never considered questionable, and they made themselves at home by sitting on the floor and staring at the TV screen, which was perched at a convenient height for their viewing pleasure. Naturally, in such salubrious circumstances, homework and studies very often took a back seat, even as visitors and their welcome to our home was given due graciousness. In summertime, the number of viewers was even greater as the TV was displayed in the open-sky area, near the small garden of the house. It was great fun.

I recall there was one visitor, a lady relative we called "Aunty Hama", who had a conservative bent of mind. She would make herself comfortable in front of the screen, but instead of viewing it, she would steal glances, covering her face behind her veil, stating that it was unbecoming of her to expose herself unveiled in front of strange men! 'The person on the TV screen speaking to all of us is looking at me,' she would retort when quizzed about her mannerism.

And once, it so happened that there was a social event in the house which coincided with the TV viewing episode. The viewers were thus treated as honourable guests on the occasion, and during the telecast, there arose the question of whether to serve the ladies or men first for dinner. Aunty Hama was among those invitees and she advocated, 'You must serve the fellow on the screen first. He must be very hungry after all that telecasting he has been doing for such a long time!' Poor lady, she was the centre of teasing and mockery from all the people present. She also took it sportively and started laughing at herself, without being convinced by our arguments, or able to remove her veil, at least at that stage.

So much for the coming together of modern technology and gastronomic hospitality.

Chapter 5

Bonding Around Food

Culinary traditions are an important part of a nation's culture and heritage. Old nations are also known for their great cuisine and variety of food. It is a source of pride to belong to one of those old nations with a strong culture and distinct identity. Morocco, a nation of more than twelve centuries, is known to have one of the top cuisines worldwide, benefiting from the melting of cross-cultures and various ethnic groups, each contributing to the richness of the country. Thus, Moroccan cuisine, for many, remains a refined, extravagant and elaborate one, capable of accommodating different tastes and budgets also. It changes from region to region, according to their weather, products of the seasons and the soil. The cuisine in the south-east of Morocco, commonly known as "Tafilalet", from where my family originates, remains a modest one in variety but generous in quantity, in comparison with the northern and western regions. Yet, it remains distinct, with few dishes specific to that part of the country, becoming a must-taste when visiting the area.

As such, the memories of childhood that I do recall time and again are the ones that are centred on the three mealtimes at our house. Usually, the cooking was part of the responsibility that my mother, along with my father's stepmother, shouldered with the girls and the domestic help. But the shopping sprees were the times when we, boys, had some contribution in getting products from the market, while accompanying, frequently, my grandfather, and later on, my father.

With three meals to prepare, the morning hours were busy in the kitchen, with the most time spent in preparing the two major meals for the day. But by 11 a.m., the morning's kitchen activities would generally be over, and the kitchen would be tidied and cleaned up. Then followed, what you might call a round of elevenses, when ladies of the neighbourhood dropped in for conversations around the customary practice of tea-drinking. There was a spread of small eats alongside, such as almonds, especially homemade cakes, and freshly baked bread. This ritual of tea and conversation was wound up, usually, before lunchtime, corresponding to the afternoon prayers.

What I most often recall of breakfast specialities at home was the delectable taste of bowls of *Harira* made either of *Dshisha* (wheat) or *Wargiya* (a kind of leaves like that of cabbage, used as a vegetable). Both were common, delicious soups, prepared alternately, unless there were special guests in the house, where the soup would take a step back and become a complement. The velvety smoothness of the soup-like dish would immediately bring upon us pangs of hunger. Its yellow-red colour, for the first, yellow-white for the second, when turmeric is added to either of them, would make both seem a thing of beauty for the eyes. And then came the actual tasting of either of them. It was thickened by a mixture known as *"tadwira"* based on wheat for *Harira* or, at times, with milk. As far as I can recall, the second would generally be for *Dshisha*. And after feasting my eyes, came the taste of fresh herbs—coriander, parsley and the sharp aftertaste of the celery leaves in the end. The meat was usually added in the *Harira*, for those who could afford it, to make it consistent, rich and highly nutritious… a complete meal in itself. That's also what explains its presence on the table, almost every day at the breaking fast time, during the holy month of Ramadan.

Here, I must stop to tell you a bit about the lamb that we consume. Usually, the lamb reared for the table is stall-fed with wheat, dry and hard dates, and highly nutritious ground date seeds full of vitamins and minerals. The most well-known and liked breed of sheep is dubbed *"Damman"* as opposed to *"Sardi"*, a breed predominant in the centre, north of Morocco and in the Atlas Mountains. In fact, the *Damman* is so carefully bred that the animal is not allowed to graze, so that the meat remains tender as the leg muscles would not be over-exercised. The diet of dates and seeds add a unique taste to it. The meat, therefore, when added to the Harira or used as kebabs, has a special "intrinsic sweetness" in its quality, as the texture of the meat is very tender.

Along with the handpicked meat, the other ingredients of the dish, too, are equally important. The basic ingredients for the *Harira* soup are made of lentils and chickpeas, to which seasonal vegetables are added. I recall that in winter, the Harira pot was thicker with added seasonal vegetables, and the entire preparation was served with bread and a choice of dates. What I now miss from that childhood taste is the absence of fava beans in the *Harira*, a vegetable that I would look for in it, and which I have not found very common in many places around the world, including India, although it is taken for granted back home. But to be honest, other soups were also available. One was called *"Mhamsa"* and the other *"Lssan Tir"*, which literally means the "bird's tongue".

Another vegetable that has always been, and still is, linked to summertime at home was a daily preparation of okra dishes called *"Mloukhiya"*. It was pleasant to consume and was prepared with meat on a very slow fire for hours. It was liked all the time, regardless of guests, who invariably dropped in. The accompaniment with okra is always *"Khobz"*, bread, which allows one to soak up the juices with the bread and enjoy the taste. We call it the "bread enemy" as whatever quantity of bread is brought, it vanishes, as if it had never existed. There are many stories behind and relating to this dish and its accompanying bread, where each one is more incredible than the other.

One of the strangest, but likely true, stories happened a long time ago, when a farmer brought his wife the first pieces of okra of the year from his farm, excited to have lunch with it when he returned from the fields in the afternoon. His wife was even more impatient to cook it and enjoy the dish with him. However, once the dish was ready, after a few hours of cooking, and since her husband would arrive much later, she decided she couldn't wait for him. Thus, she took her share and left her husband's for later, when he would come back. But after having eaten her half, her hands couldn't stop as her mouth was asking for more and more of this incredible dish. She never imagined she would finish it all, nor did she expect what was waiting for her. Once the man of the house was back home, forgetting how his paces had covered the distance, eager as he was to eat this long-awaited favourite dish, and even feigning about it all the way, he ordered his wife to serve him the dish, at once.

Her voice was trembling, and she was hiding behind the pillars, as if feeling ashamed. Unable to decipher her behaviour, her husband was perplexed and curious to know what had happened. At his inquisition, she left the room running, only to return after gathering her energy and courage. Then she said, in a barely audible voice, 'There is no more okra for today!'

'Why is that? What happened? Did it burn over? Just bring me what has remained.'

'I said, there is simply no okra,' she repeated as if she had been reporting a catastrophe that had occurred. It was, at least for him.

'It has all gone. I had my half, but the bread took the other half—your half,' she murmured.

The man could not believe what he heard and burst into an uncontrolled anger, shouting his lungs out at her, even raining all kinds of insults upon her.

'Well,' he said, 'the first half was yours, fair enough, but the second one—I mean mine—why and how did it vanish?'

No word was strong enough to convey his frustration. Then, without thinking twice, he said, 'You can no longer be trusted and, as such, there is no more place for you in this household.'

The sentence was executed immediately.

If for many, this was a true story, which I could not confirm, for others, it was an exaggerated tale. Whatever the truth may be, the story shows the importance this dish had, and still has, in the daily life of the people of the region of Tafilalet, who are truly and literally "addicted" to it, mainly during the summer season.

Later on, *Couscous* became the much-anticipated dish on Fridays. The dish was consumed in a leisurely fashion with our cousins, as on that day, one had more time on hand, owing to Friday prayers, to relish what was served. I recall how we all sat together around the table. Finally, meals were usually rounded off with servings of either melons, watermelons, figs, grapes or apricots in summertime, and oranges and apples, among other fruits, in other seasons. The dessert dish would comprise, at times of more than one kind of fruit, especially in the presence of guests. Most of the fruits were produced in the region, and others from other parts of Morocco, except for bananas, which were imported, until more than two decades ago, when they started to be produced locally, along with a few other tropical origin fruits.

Looking back over time, I now realise the care that was taken at home, not just in making the food, but also the ritual of shopping for the ingredients needed to prepare the food. Also, food was not rationed out into family portions only. Guests would arrive at our home as a matter of course. It was not customary for them to inform us about their coming beforehand. Besides, Father being in the administration meant that guests arrived at lunchtime either from the market or after completion of their business in different administrations and government offices. Whatever the reason behind their coming, food for them was a ritual taken for granted. After all, isn't generosity about caring and sharing genuinely?

Hence, the shopping routine for food items was an important activity at home. Rissani boasted the richest and more elaborate marketplace in and around the area and was well supplied with fruit and vegetables. Few vegetables were locally grown, but most of the stock would arrive fresh to the market initially from Casablanca, the economic capital, located at some 750 km away, and later on from Meknes, at 450 km from my town. The produce would be delivered in lorries every second day, and customers would arrive in large numbers from all over the area. Thus, market days of the household were on Tuesdays, Thursdays and Sundays, as they were the days which coincided with the truck supply days.

Thinking back in memory of my region, I also recall that market days were not just for mundane shopping sprees. They were also exciting because of the many sights and sounds that were linked to my childhood memories. The bargain offers doing the rounds at the shops still echo in my ears. Indeed, the brisk trade at the butcher shops and, above all, the busy atmosphere in and around the bakeries in Rissani are dear memories that cannot be forgotten easily.

My region is also and especially known for its signature baked bread known as the *"Medfouna"*, which is essentially a circular-shaped dough that is rolled out and then filled. I remember the variety of ingredients that went—and still go—into it…. Though it could be arranged and made at home, the preparation for this special, appetising and rich meal was prepared entirely outside, in specialised bakeries. The ladies would always encourage and be happy to have it made at the bakeries for the reasons you certainly know. In fact there were very few restaurants available, and they were basically used by tourists and outsiders. Also, it was not easily acceptable, culturally, for people having their homes and families or friends there, to eat outside. Therefore, the *Medfouna*, also called the pizza of the desert, would allow the housewives to relax and enjoy a meal they were not responsible for making, nor would they take the trouble to prepare. Somehow, it was like being guests in their own home—a situation they would want to renew and live in, as often as they could.

As far as its preparation goes, once the dough has risen, it is rolled out. Meat was filleted into kebab-sized portions, as also boiled eggs, almonds, onions, herbs, and spices were layered onto the round. It was then covered with another round, and the sides were pinched together. It was then taken to the local baker, and eaten piping hot—either at homes for the locals or at one of the cafés or restaurants. A small extra amount could be charged to customers for booking a table without ordering any food from the restaurant. The feast would not be complete without being accompanied by strong, hot Moroccan mint tea. I also remember how the sides were designed into a fluted pattern that puffed up into a light brown colour when the bread came out of the oven.

The *Medfouna* became—and remains to this day—a must for any visitor to Rissani.

And of course, the highlight of the food calendar for a child like me was the occasional wedding feasts in the family. The invitees I recall vividly were my maternal uncles and aunts who would arrive with their families, and this swelled the numbers to around one hundred guests. Besides them, there were other relatives and altogether the extended family, I imagine, counted up to two hundred and more! The food would be laid out on a good number of tables, with each table seating a group of eight to ten guests. On the sides of each table were those colourful plates of salads, and all the guests would arrange themselves when the food was about to be served. Men and women would be served separately; men usually proceeded to resume their work while ladies would extend the afternoon till the fall of the night. Usually, there wouldn't be less than two dishes of meat and chicken preparations, and, at times, you may get another course of *Couscous*, not with vegetables, but rather with sugar and cinnamon. Whatever the set-up that was made, the guests would partake of that hearty feast with relish.

And then there is another set of happenings which I would like to include in my list of foods and activities around it. These were the times when relatives would arrive with their family members to spend the school holidays. They would arrive without any prior announcement to relax with us at our home. These were families of uncles and aunts from my mother's and father's sides who would come in this manner. There were also non-relative guests who would come on business visits. They, too, were welcomed and added to the *hoi polloi* of the home and truly helped me live the holiday spirit. Conversely, we would also visit family members in other cities, mainly Fes, Meknes or Rabat, and the same spirit of hearty welcoming would prevail. How easy, simple, and enjoyable life was! We all cherished being reunited and together, without complications or calculations, regardless of the size of the place where we were. All enjoyed the company of their peers, younger or older. Oh, how I long for those bygone days

Looking back, I now realise that all this added up to plenty of festivities, big and small, that happened all through childhood. That they were occasions that had been made unique to us is clear from the fact that they have stayed on in memory and can still bring back a smile, over all this passage of time. For us children, all the houses in the neighbourhood were ours, and whenever we felt a hollow in our stomach, we would enter the nearest house and be served whatever was available, without bothering to go home. It was quite natural in our minds that all the mothers and fathers were somehow like ours and received the same respect. Everybody was an educator and would care for the other children as theirs. How wonderful in its simplicity it was, that feeling of solidarity, care, and love.

Going beyond just homely fare and family, the country, too, has its fair share of festival alternatives. One of these is the annual calendar of food festivals centred around the fruits that are native to the different regions of Morocco. Special times were thus earmarked in different cities for holding what is called a "festival around a fruit". Sure enough, in the vicinity of Rissani, we too featured in this festive calendar, associated with the annual "dates" festival at Erfoud near Rissani, and which is said to be the best supply of dates in the country. Then, of course, there are others, like the Festival of Cherries close to Fes in the region of Sefrou, which abounds in cherry trees. The blossoming trees yield a rich harvest in May–June, making this occasion a feast for the senses, with plenty of the fruit available, as also dancing and singing and Fantasia Shows—celebrating victory, during the bygone days—giving the whole atmosphere the trappings of a timeless tradition. I must also include the festival of apples, too, because that fruit has the best production of all of Morocco's fruits, especially from the Atlas Mountains' cold region around Midelt. All these festivals, and many more in other places, have had their elected queens, carefully chosen from among the local girls.

At times, I have tried to apply a little logic of my own to identify why it is that the tastes of my childhood have continued to linger in my mouth even today. The answer I have deciphered, though a personal one, is that the ingredients which were grown and nurtured on the Mediterranean soil, in my humble opinion, remain one of the best on Earth. And the cooking medium for them is the olive oil from that big area in the south and north of the Mediterranean Sea, which I can vouch for, is the best olive oil in the world! Hence, it is the unique combination of the Sun, the water, and the soil of my land that has been the actual source of contentment behind all those childhood meals.

Last but not least is a "feast" that deserves to be honoured with feasts, in terms of the best understanding of the word. It was our weekly holiday from school every Saturday. That day was nothing short of a feast, because we could stay in our beds and not have to get up early to prepare for going to school, especially in the very cold winters of the semi-arid area where we used to belong, in the South-East of Morocco. No one came along to remind us that we must get up, except my father, who, at times, would feel lonely as he used to get up early, and would disturb this indescribable quietude. Sheer bliss, that I definitely like to savour many times over!

Chapter 6

Life's Best Educators

The wisdom of hindsight, by which I look back to my earliest school years, has made me realise how these are not merely interwoven with imbibing just the 3R's of education (reading, writing, and arithmetic), but are rather rooted in behavioural foundations that have remained with me today, as life lessons shaping my entire persona. Perhaps the most important of these educational milestones was my attitude towards my teachers. Perceptively, I find that the teachers who bestowed upon me the largesse of learning and education, in the broader sense of life lessons, have remained constant and unchanged in my estimation of them. I still feel the same respect towards them that I had felt when I was a child in their care.

Incidentally, this feeling has always been with me. At the sight of any of my early teachers, the innocent schoolboy that I had been would take over the person I was, almost instantly. This was put to the test in quite an unplanned way, a few years back. I was then serving as Head of the Asia Directorate in the Moroccan Ministry of Foreign Affairs and Cooperation. I had to go to Meknes because my mother's sister had passed away, and the gathering of relatives and friends paying condolences was taking place at my eldest uncle's home. People were filing past, conveying their sympathies in our bereavement, when I noticed that Mr Moufid, my first Arabic teacher at primary school, had also come for the occasion.

Apart from more grey hair covering his head, my early teacher looked exactly the same in height and shape, down to his small spectacles. When our eyes met, I felt as if time had stopped for a while, transporting me more than forty-five years back. My spontaneous reaction on seeing him was entirely natural and intrinsically genuine. Almost on impulse, I took his hand to kiss it—the same way I had been used to doing earlier for my teachers and equally for my parents and elders. In fact, I can't imagine, even now, greeting my maternal uncles and other elders without kissing their hands. This habit has grown with me and, somehow, I am proud that I have never tried to avoid it. Deep within myself, I like it this way. It keeps me as I have been in their eyes for a long time, despite my current social status. I am happy to be tagged as a man who keeps real values.

Returning to Mr Moufid—his immediate reaction was to pull my hand back firmly, probably because he felt that I had now grown up and was a man of position in society and thus he, a retired humble primary school teacher, should not be the recipient of such courtesies from a pupil who had been in his charge in the early school years. For me, on the contrary, the years were sloughed away and the matter of my official position was not in the least a consideration at that moment, nor should it be, ever. My behaviour towards him was exactly the same as it had been, as a six-year-old pupil, when I would kiss his hand and pay him due respect, regardless of whether the encounter was at school or outside. Didn't we learn that a teacher could have been a prophet, as their primary mission was to educate and show the right path to the learners of many generations?

For a while, the incident became quite a crowd distracter as I insisted on kissing his hand, and he, on the other hand, stood his ground and vehemently tried to deny me the opportunity of paying my respects to him. On the contrary, he was trying to do it reversely —by pulling my hand firmly to kiss it. It was his way to show how he was proud of me. I would never allow it, of course. This tussle persisted until I found a solution—by climbing onto the sofa and requesting him to allow me to kiss his forehead at least, by way of a gesture, to publicly recognise the institution he represented and to express, almost instinctively, my thankfulness and gratitude for him and, through him, to all my teachers and educators. At first, he was reluctant, but gave in upon my insistence and went on adding, emotionally, with slightly wet eyes, 'It is pupils like you who make a teacher feel proud.' We both ended up like two old ladies from my hometown, when they met after a while and expressed their love by alternately kissing each other's hands almost endlessly.

What he, and all the other teachers who came after him, had imbibed in me is what lingers on in my persona. Yes, on the one hand, it was this deep-seated respect for the giver of education, but on another, and at a still deeper level, they had taught me that the value of things in life is unchangeable. It is the price of a commodity that is changeable, and I must not confuse the two distinct identities of present-day circumstances with those of a person's current social status in life. We were taught at home to accept everyone regardless of skin colour, status, abilities, or disabilities, and so on. I was fortunate to have had teachers like Mr Moufid who were accepting, rather than demarcating, and used group work with a variety of students, thus encouraging collaboration in the true sense of the term, long before it became a buzzword in the corridors of educational institutions.

This same attitude of giving respect where it was due, I must acknowledge, was reinforced at our home, too. As is wont, due to my father's position, we had the comfort of always having servants to attend to our needs and help in the household. But the discipline of the house demanded that we not demean them, imagining that they occupied an inferior status in comparison to us. We were taught to greet them with respect and even kiss their hands, mainly after getting back from school, as my father would repeat: 'Don't have this confusion in your minds that you can ignore their status. They are paid for what they do. Yes, the pay they receive to serve any of us does not give you the right to not respect them, at least for their age. Besides, our situation could have been easily and reversely theirs.' Something, I and, I am sure, my brothers and sisters, did not understand, at least at that age, and would contest discreetly.

In our tender years, it is clear to me in hindsight that we had all the ingredients in our home set-up to become spoiled and prone to self-gratification. My father's official status provided a conduit for people to curry favour with the son of the highest authority in town, but Father took every opportunity to impress upon us that such advantages and positions were not permanent. 'People are born free and they are serving the community; so should we all,' was his constant teaching. Right from an early age, therefore, we were taught to regard the underlying value of things and not to gloat over the price of things. These were embedded so sternly, through actions and deeds rather than words, that they have become second nature for me.

But there were irresistible distractions at times that did not allow me to practise what was preached to me, particularly in the matter of watches. Right from an early age, I had an uncommon fascination for watches, but instead of taking care of these timepieces, my passion lay in unscrewing the watch and examining the mechanism under the cover. Hence, as I mentioned earlier, every watch that I could lay my hands on was promptly and surreptitiously whisked off to the washroom. There, in the peace and the secrecy of that space, whenever a watch lost accuracy, I would undo the tiny screws and look within, at the ticking mechanism, in wide-eyed wonder, believing I could repair it. I was so engrossed with this act that, whenever I heard a noise or a knock at the door, I would not take the trouble of arranging out the screws in proper order, so that I could screw back the parts and make the watch whole again. Inevitably, the watches that landed in my hands met their doomsday. Only the "blessed" ones had the good fortune of escaping the fate of being botched up completely and beyond repair. These lucky escapees, of course, were few and far between.

Back to the school routine, I now recall that, like the watches, there were two categories of subjects—and this division was made not by the school authorities but by *yours truly*. Though the official ruling was that pupils were being taught grammar, composition and reading, languages (Arabic, then French after the first two years), civics, and arithmetic to qualify for the "Certificate *d'Études* Primaires" or CM2, I had my own yardstick of preferences. As a flashback, I now remember that what I was taught at school during the tertiary years were demarcated into those that were upgraded to a position of being "liked" by me, and others that were summarily dismissed as unfit for my scholarly tastes or preferences, and doomed for abandonment, while the likeable subjects, like the lucky watches, were born to leave behind a mark.

For me personally, the subjects that were elevated to a position of acceptance were the study of our history and geography. Of the two, it was geography that took the upper hand, as even at that early age, I was fascinated with the idea of travelling to distant lands and seeing the many facets of the world, starting with Morocco itself. It appeared to me that these geographic travels equalled the story of my country and gave me a sense of pride, making me long for more. In primary school, too, I was enchanted with poetry recitation. Perhaps it was the rhythmic nature of the verses that caught my schoolboy's imagination and kept me engrossed.

The history lessons, on the other hand, entered via a vicarious path and became an extension from an outside source, which was not strictly classroom-related. It was through the many stories that I heard at home. In those days, a midwife lived mostly as a resident in our family, as she was considered a full member, and discharged her duties of providing health education to my mother on nutrition during pregnancy and lactation, and other sundry matters of the family. Her son was brought up mostly at home and stayed with us as a member of the family as well. But besides that, "Lalla Ftim Ali", as she was commonly called, took a great deal of interest in us, the younger family members, by becoming a gifted storyteller. I recollect how we gathered round her in the kitchen premises and listened wide-eyed and agog at the escapades of mythical beings, magic wonders, and charming emperors, and so on… all the while imbibing the lore of history through her dramatic presentations.

In fact, her fascinating narration was so gripping that we often lay down, covered by blankets, and fell asleep in the kitchen, where she usually sat and where we all preferred to be, especially in wintertime. The warmth of the fire and the imagery of those stories in the twilight and night were like a soporific for us. Cannily enough, the stories this motherly figure in our household told us each night always ended with some life lesson in tow, or a piece of wisdom, and this aspect ingrained itself unconsciously in our psyche.

Overall, my early schooling was quite a modest one, in terms of facilities and privileges. I now recall that there was no arrangement, to speak of, for organised sports like team games at the school. The schools at that time were often not well-equipped for such luxuries, although I recall that our primary school had a big courtyard with only the alleys to and between classrooms, which were paved with stones. At break times, we used to play football but very frequently, the ball would hit the classroom windows, which spoiled the fun of the game and led to collective punishment.

While the incident provided an amusing aside, it was not the only entertainment that I remember over the years. There were those enjoyable school functions, where we pupils played very decisive roles. We were trained to enact small dramas or epics on the occasion of the Enthronement Day, which was celebrated on the third of March each year, during the reign of the previous King, late Hassan II, the father of the current King, Mohammed VI. It was a fiercely competitive event, and every school did a great deal of preparation for it. I recall that practices for it began in early January. The entire school, boys and girls, would be involved in some role and made us realise the importance of that day in our national history, right at an early age.

Of course, there was the reverse side of the coin, too. While I was in the final year of my primary school, we shifted to a bigger city called Erfoud, twenty kilometres away from my hometown, Rissani, as my father had been reappointed there, with a bigger responsibility. However, my parents, wanting to ensure a certain stability for my studies, decided, with my full consent and even enthusiasm, to send me to Rabat, for middle school studies, as a hardly eleven-year-old boy, despite the fact that Erfoud had a well-reputed secondary school. This was also because we all thought the area where we resided held fewer opportunities and prospects for those who wanted to better their lives and have a higher quality education than our area. At least so did I believe at that time.

Rabat had always been associated, for me and my siblings, with the holidays we used to spend together, now and then, as a family, at my eldest paternal uncle's house, during summertime. The sun, stretched beaches, no restrictions, no early getting-up hassles, and plenty of places to spend leisure time, have fun, and good times. I was wrong. None of these things was possible to enjoy during the school period. It was a mirage and a total disappointment for a child of my age then.

This change from my home environment at my tender age had, for sure, a negative trail. The separation of almost 600 kilometres from my nearest kith and kin, particularly from my mother, at an age when I would need her most for a little support, made me react in an unbecoming way. Most of the time, my uncle used to share his house with another, slightly distant, cousin with the same family name. He was a secondary-school Arabic teacher. The nursemaid, Hnia, who attended to my uncles' comforts and to mine after joining them, such as maintaining clothes, cleaning, and cooking meals, became the target of my illogical dislike. Subconsciously, I felt that she had usurped my mother's place in my life and, though she doted on me and made sure that all my needs were taken care of, I was often reluctant to accept her care with gratitude, for no apparent reason.

At school, my results were declining, and I was losing interest in the whole exercise. Surprisingly, it seemed to me that quality education in my hometown was far better than what I was expecting to receive in Rabat. Of course, my judgement was far from being accurate, as my mind was distracted elsewhere, and I was refusing to admit I was unprepared for all this sudden and big change. My sole concern was to count the days and wait eagerly for holidays to return home. I remember how my poor uncle was very upset with me and took my inability to cope with the life he was offering me as his personal failure. That "heavy" responsibility, he couldn't assume for long, disturbed him visibly, especially after having assured my father he would manage my stay and education, without difficulty. He had never expected that the soft and kind boy he used to meet in the summer holidays would give him such big and unjustified trouble. My overall stay there did not last more than two years. My uncle and parents concluded that if I were not back home and put in a boarding school, they might lose me completely as I was on the verge of ruining my life… a "failure" which my uncle was not prepared to assume for the rest of his life. Yet, I didn't have the slightest doubt that he did all he could to make my stay as comfortable and rewarding as possible. I was the problem, not him. So, not only did I have to admit this bitter reality, but I also had to make it known to my parents to free both his and my conscience. I couldn't afford to lose either him or myself.

Over the years, it is these fragments of sweet and bitter memories that have become valuable souvenirs. They are the charming keepsakes of my social, cognitive, cultural, emotional, and physical growth treasures. They are, in a way, the movers and shakers of future attitudes and abilities. Of course, I did not consciously acquire these aptitudes, but I learnt what it is to be a man, to assume responsibility at an early age, to interact beyond the home and to be a cautiously alert person. Indeed, travelling alone in different buses, with at least one change in one city—if not two—ingrained in me the ability to assume responsibility, the responsibility of myself, and the alertness to remain cautious of any potential threat or danger for the small boy that I was.

I presume that all those moments—ups and downs—made me understand the big difference between having a house, however comfortable it may be, and a sweet home. It also helped me appreciate the value of family and friends. Unfortunately, many of those friends from my early years have been erased from my physical spaces because of my father's frequent mobility and, later on, my own higher studies. My job didn't help in solving this equation, but it made it worse. However, the entity that was school, along with the laughable and not-so-laughable sides, contributed to assembling lifelong learning lessons that have shaped my personality into the persona that I am.

Chapter 7

Path Readjustment

I am structurally a fatalistic person, and I strongly believe in destiny. I may have had this conviction from my religion and family background, and also from observing the lives of the others around me, and that of myself. Yet, there are decisions and events that come in the course of each one's life that may change it considerably either way. If you are lucky, then the change is positive; otherwise, it can take a complete turn—a one-eighty-degree shift in the opposite direction. In the latter case, what would be required is to readjust so that the consequences would remain at their minimum level.

My first two years of studies in secondary school in the Moroccan capital could be seen through this perspective, and it worked both ways. Indeed, in the mind of a boy of less than eleven, who I was, Rabat was the embodiment of fun and good times that we enjoyed during summer holidays. Hence, Rabat was synonymous with endless fun, balmy weather, and a sense of utter abandon in every aspect. I had therefore accepted—without hesitation and in my full awareness—my father's proposal, or rather decision, made overnight, to shift me to Rabat for studies, where I would reside with my uncle. I was attending the Tadili Secondary School, in Bab Lhad Square, at the heart of the city. The gate of my school, a fifteen-minute walk from home, was exactly at the opposite end of the main entrance to the Jewish Cemetery and just a few steps away from the bus stations—one for inter-city travels and the other for urban transport.

Alas! Rabat's pleasure quotient, as I mentioned earlier, was rudely shaken by this new association as a place of lessons and school regimen, instead of carefree summer holidays. In short, I could not adjust to this changeover and, although my uncle, Mehdi, along with the lady caretaker, Hnia, had done their utmost for my comfort, I was miserable and lost, to say the least. Looking back in hindsight, I find that it was probably my tender age which refused to accept another individual as a caregiver in place of my mother, and the sum total of events was that I was in for a complete free fall, without any reins to stop the downslide. In these circumstances, my father, as a knowing elder, had made a profound decision, which I feel, to this day, was instrumental in changing me from boyhood to manhood, from an indifferent learner to a studious and committed one, from the 'proverbial disoriented young boy' into a well-adjusted individual entering the teenage years with more assurance.

On the home front, too, there had been disruptions of sorts. My father had been shifted to another posting, to Jorf, and as a family we were residing twenty kilometres away from the town of Erfoud, where I had to pursue my studies at the En-Nakhil College, which had a large boarding school. Personally, too, the change came as a welcome alternative, and now that I look back on those days, I realise that it was a heaven-sent opportunity for me and my future, as I owe my persona and upbringing, to a large extent, to the years of schooling I had been privileged to imbibe there. The principal of the boarding school was a friend of my father's, and I was sent there because we all were convinced that it was the best choice for equipping me with an environment where there was a regulated upbringing as well as the opportunity for me to cope with my academics.

In broad terms, I will not hesitate to say that this college had a boarding school unlike any other. However, as I reckon the whole thing over, again and again, I have often wondered how the administration had striven to make the environment strict—a military-like regime—but also working towards the good of the pupils. What I discovered from the school environment is that if one was reasonably good, precocious enough, and overall serious enough, then this establishment was the ideal educator. In my personal capacity, I pay a deep-seated tribute to this gentleman, the responsible head, in charge of managing the boarding school, not just for how he shaped me and moulded my future, but also for the fact that, like me, he saved so many other souls. His name was Haj Terfass. We were used to calling him Uncle L'Haj. Somehow, in comparison, the meaning of his name suited his kind. Incidentally, *Terfass* in Moroccan Arabic means the desert truffle, which has its goodness hidden below the ground and which needs to be extricated and partaken, to understand its worth. Indeed, he was unique in all aspects.

Before I go any further, I must draw attention to the principles on which the foundations of the school's overall culture were based. Though we came from different backgrounds, at the school we lived as one community, with equal chances, responsibilities and care. The sole aim of our education was to push us to study to the uppermost limit of our capacity, and there were no concessions made for anyone, where no one was favoured on account of the social or financial status, or personal get-up, or other exterior divisive factors. We learnt to value each other for who we were as individuals, and certainly not for where we came from.

I realise now, while looking back, that the runaway success of this institution lies in shaping and saving so many teenage souls. On a lighter note, we youngsters quipped that L'Haj was like the legendary *"Jinn"*—as he was invisible yet present everywhere, literally everywhere, at all times—and seemed to have a hidden camera-like focus, recording all the happenings at school and outside. His standards of expectation from individual pupils, under his responsibility at the boarding school, were driven by an unfaltering dedication to push every pupil to their maximum capacity. He made use of times when we students were engaged in group-based activities, such as, when we were queued up like soldiers to get into the dining hall for lunch. I recall his calling me, or any other person, out and chiding me physically, leaving me and the entire hundreds alike rather nonplussed. The next minute, his action sank in, as he would say... 'Maliki—come here! What is your name?' We all knew that it was useless to argue or retort. He would continue, rather mockingly, addressing everybody through the person before him like a hearing in a court: 'Look at you, I don't understand how a person like you, who has the chance that thousands of your ilk don't, and still no good results or prospects in studies. You can leave your seat for a more deserving one if you can't cope with the school exigencies. We don't need people like you here. The Government provides you with food, shelter, education and so on. Then why aren't you among the top ones of your class?' Sometimes ironically, the unlucky person concerned may be at the top of his class, or good enough not to deserve such a stressful situation. We all would think that if he did this to a brilliant student, what would he do to a lesser one!

But that was how he encouraged everyone to do more, including the already good ones. Our results represented for him the mirror through which people and parents would judge the entire school, but mainly his work and dedication to the job. He was intractable on this. In later years, I have realised that, what would obviously appear to be a rather high-handed and illogical way of encouraging children, was his unique and special way of making us exert to make the best use of our potential and push it to the limit. This would push to frown at remaining mediocre learners, who would lose out on opportunities, simply because they had not been taught to use their innate capacities a little bit further…

At this stage, I must make it clear that he did not single out any person to make an example of their inertia and ignorance of their potential. The entire school was run like clockwork—or a well-oiled paramilitary environment. Lights were off at 9 o'clock, regardless of the situation. We used to wake up at five in the morning, during exam periods, and at six on normal days. Breakfast was served at 7.30 a.m. sharp each day, and there were always the same things on the table: bread, butter, or cheese, on rare occasions, then jam and, of course, what would resemble coffee, served in fat, round and transparent glasses. The combination of all these elements made it a very tasty meal of the morning. But again, did we have any better option?

The regime made it possible for Uncle L'Haj to manage a school of more than three hundred young adults like his own home, regardless of the numbers. The youngest of us was between eleven and twelve years, and the senior ones, preparing for the Baccalaureate Exams, were eighteen to twenty-three years of age. They were old enough to be thinking, already, of either future careers or pursuing further studies at university and higher institutions.

Such wide age variations are also beset with inbuilt problems. This institution was no exception in this regard. Among many incidents that happened during the five years I spent there, there is one which I recall vividly. It concerned an attempted sexual abuse of one of the younger children by the older boys, who were taken up with his good looks, shyness, and kindness. Instead of just dealing with the culprits individually and sparing the rest of us from knowledge about this sordid affair, Uncle L'Haj had rightly made a severely corrective scheme, making this incident a lesson and an example of personal behaviour for each and every pupil in his charge.

A trap was laid at night. The victim was ordered to look for a shelter outside school for the night and not to retire to his usual bed. Instead, it was the principal who had laid down in his place. When the lights were off, nobody knew how he sneaked and lay down in the bed of the boy. He was covering himself with a thick *lhaf* or cover, as it was in the middle of winter, waiting for the culprits to show up one by one. He used to have a beard linked to his moustache in a zero-like form with a bit of white hair, resembling the layer of snow on dark mountainous rocks in early spring. It was his signature, and you wouldn't miss him by any means. The unsuspecting predators came and announced their names, little realising that it was L'Haj himself who was putting the query from under the thick coverlet. The next moment, the offender's hand was held, and Uncle L'Haj would take it to his beard. In order not to be discovered by the neighbouring sleepers, or to alert the others who would come for the night adventure, his unmistakable thundering voice, slow, now, like a whisper, would ask the trapped chap, 'You know who I am!' Of course he would, and he should.

Once he knew that the wrongdoer had got the fright and surprise of his life, he would order him to go and report to his office and wait there. He would do it repeatedly until steps were no longer heard and all voices faded in the dark dormitory, except for some snores here and there. In this manner, he had rounded up the gang, and the aftermath of the incident was played out in full, with the boys being boxed to a virtual state of unconsciousness, all the while having it dinned into their heads that they had come to this institution to study and nothing else. Hardly did we know who the culprits were, as their identities were not revealed by the principal. However, we could suspect who they were—or at least a few of them. The incident had its expected sobering effect, and since then we wouldn't hear of even minor episodes of bullying, misdeeds, abuses or maltreatments at the boarding school, for a long time. I suppose, nevertheless, that this habit may have continued after the incident, as may be the case in many other similar institutions worldwide.

On the other hand, there was undoubtedly an inbuilt advantage to having boys of different ages under a single roof. One could seek advice from the older boys, and the study atmosphere certainly got a boost, as the younger ones looked up to their studious seniors and saw how their efforts yielded positive results. After all, it was an era prior to the current culture of messaging and emails. Face-to-face discussions were the norm. Oh, how I pity the youngsters of this time for not enjoying such unique moments of communion and real friendships instead of the commonly current norm of virtual and ephemeral ones. Also, there was a regulated study hour routine for scholars daily, both in the morning and during evening hours, which was supervised—generally by senior students—and one could obtain help if required from the other students of different levels of study. During exam periods, another study time was imposed between morning and afternoon classes, straight after lunch. These study classes were monitored by what we called boarding school supervisors, who would control the presence and report any absence, irregularities or misuse of the time allocated to schoolwork and learning.

But there were digressions too. I was pushed to believe, wrongly, how fascinating and adult assertive it was to smoke. In our free time, we used to go out discreetly for some fresh air with selected friends, mainly from my home town. Few of them used to smoke, and I was tempted, though moderately, to do the same. One day, Uncle L'Haj got to know about it and, of course, reported it to his friend, my father. It was a true disgrace for me. I can't remember it even now without reviving that feeling of shame. When my mother discovered this bad habit, she was outraged to the point of insane reactions and fury. She threw everything that lay within reach of her hands at me. She backed it up with angry tirades, reminding me that I was the sole deviant, as none of my uncles nor any of my siblings had indulged in such wrongdoing, which she even qualified as a sin.

It was the wrong thing to do in my family, from an education and manners point of view—especially at that time. As the eldest son, there was a feeling that I might lead my younger siblings on the path of doom and destruction, and that the entire family and its reputation were stained forever! But my father had a more sobering and corrective approach. A few days after he had been informed about it, and while visiting home in Jorf, during a short vacation, he asked me to join him in the office in the late afternoon. Meanwhile, I was restless, wondering what form his reaction—or punishment—would take. I knew there would be one, and somehow believed also, there should be. Deep in my soul, I was convinced that I deserved a severe reprimand. I waited for a long time, in front of his office before he requested his guard to usher me in at the end of the day. He sat me down before him and instead of resorting, as I was expecting, to any kind of physical violence or action, he addressed me as man to man, an elder to a youngster, not as I was used to, on previous occasions.

With eyes fixated on me and in a deep voice, he said: 'It is not for me to ask you to smoke or to stop smoking. You are grown up and you must know where your interests lie and what you want to achieve in life, success or failure. But I find it rather a shame, even weird, that you use the money I give you—for books, studies, and to cover your basic and urgent needs—on cigarettes. It is simply unacceptable. When you are grown up and become a man in the real sense, earning your own money from proper sweating, only then I would not have any objection or say on how you spend it—whether you want to use it on smoking or drinking or any such indulgence. But as long as you rely on my hard-earned money only to use it for such things, I certainly do have a say in the matter and still have the right to check how it is used—or misused.' The meeting was over, short, but I felt time stopped and inner sweat was being built. I didn't say a word apart from the regrets I tried to convey by murmuring. I am not sure if they were audible enough to reach his ears.

My father had a very strong personality, and standing before him after a wrongdoing was simply unbearable. I'll let you imagine how great a relief it was to leave his office and breathe fresh air. Yet, his words were deeply scathing. For quite a few weeks after that, I could not look him in the eyes, for I felt wretched at having squandered the fruits of his labours in ways that were wholly unbecoming of me. Having in mind my previous failure in studies when I was in Rabat, I felt I had betrayed, another time, the trust Father had bestowed on me. As his eldest son, I felt that by not orienting my life in the right direction, I was not just hurting myself but had done something for which I could not even forgive myself. Smoking may look so banal today for many, but at that time, it was anything but normal, and one had to take great care not to be discovered or seen smoking, mainly by elders.

So far, my recollections of my Erfoud experiences might seem rather stoic and monastic to the reader. But I would like to add that there was an equal proportion of fun activities too, injected into the school regimen. For instance, the happiest incident for most of us was the period which marked *"le Père Cent"*—which literally means 'the father of one hundred'. It was a festival we used to celebrate, as final year college students, before exactly one hundred days of undertaking the Baccalaureate examinations, the precious certificate that gives you access to institutes and universities for higher studies. We seniors would go on a fundraising campaign for the occasion, and the subscriptions were generated from the numerous administrations and shops, both in Erfoud and in the neighbouring cities. These shops willingly doled out small amounts to humour us, when I decided to enhance our core funds by using a simple, but effective trick.

We were divided into different groups for fundraising. Each group had three people for the sake of transparency. We would also ensure that each group had a male and a female. My group included two girls besides me. While collecting funds, our strategy was to keep two recording registers simultaneously. The idea behind this was to drop into the rival shops and adopt the business stance of pitching one against the other. We would show the register which had a higher contribution to enhance more from the competitive shop owner. The opening bid would be that the other shop had given a higher amount, and surely it was becoming of them to augment the contributions of their rivals, because they would be seen as more important and generous. In this way, our funds had really swelled and so had our spirits as we were in the capacity of organising many activities, including a show, and even a trip, for a few days, to many cities in the country. But the most important and featured event was the show, followed by a reception we would organise and to which many dignitaries and family members were invited. We were taking our show seriously, and would spend hours repeating and exercising what we would present on Day "D".

I recall the audience attending the show included my father, who was sitting in the audience in the first row as one of the important invitees from among the local authorities, as a parent of a final-year student, which I am sure gave him pride, like all parents present for the occasion. When I came on stage as a musician-artist playing the *"darbuka* drums" in the orchestra, I was a bit self-conscious, as he looked, to say the least, surprised, making me feel quite uncomfortable. Therefore, the only thing I had to do was to keep avoiding his gaze so as not to lose concentration during my performance on stage. After the show, while exchanging pleasantries with the instructors, he remarked that he had sent his son to the school to get an education and was surprised and didn't expect at all to see that his son was turning into a *"zeffane"*—a local mocking word to mean a local musician! But that was said in good humour, though it didn't conceal a cynical pitch in it. I assured him that he didn't have to worry about the outcome of my studies, and the event was only a window of fun and amusement before the countdown to the exam started. And my recollection of the moment was the enjoyment that we had mustered in the togetherness, in the sense of achievement at doing a job in unison and in having our friendships reinforced in the bargain!

All these incidents and experiences narrated so far, from my Erfoud days, have the merit of changing me. True, it is to say that they are good memory jerkers, but on closer reflection, I would like to add that, in my alter ego, their recall has a deeper significance as it has impacted my overall perception of other human beings. People are what they represent, in terms of values and consideration for others. Those years taught me life lessons, such as respect for people around me, without any reference or prejudice to their social status. As children of a prominent family, my brothers and I were often perceived as the gifted ones, being "sons of the *Caid* or Commissioner", often the highest administrative authority in the city. But with my social grounding at school, I was happy and comfortable to have succeeded spontaneously in coping with people as men and women and that it was only the arrogant who nourished the error of thinking themselves distinguished by extrinsic trappings. We are ultimately all the same people with different missions on Earth, and our backgrounds and education either help us reach the assigned objective, or miss it. The clue for me has always been to melt into the group and be myself as much as I can. It is a simple recipe that has worked almost always for me, and I believe it would also work for anyone when it comes as a natural behaviour and not as an adopted conduct, of course.

Chapter 8

Academic Track

When I became a Senior Secondary student at High School, where I had a good number of friends, most of us living together for years under the same ceiling in the boarding school of En-Akhil in Erfoud, a common topic of discussion among us boys, in free time or before sleeping, was about our perspectives, future plans, possible careers, and options available in the future. This was one of the most pleasant subjects we would talk about extensively and frequently, as it married the wishes and apprehensions of the realities on the ground. We would free our imagination, ruminate over what we aspired to become as adults, as we all do, at a certain stage in our lives.

As far as I can remember, I was set on my goals, at least within myself: I would work on being either a university professor or a diplomat. My father wanted me to follow his path and be in the Ministry of Interior or in one of the intelligence agencies. However, having seen how his life and ours were, because of the multiple constraints of his job, I decided to not even consider it. When we argued together on this, I would use one of his favourite adages: 'both the cow and its calf are in the mud', showing him

I didn't want to lead his life, despite the prestige, authority, and advantages it offered. This debate, which would come up, now and then, didn't change my mind an iota.

Back to my own preferences, the former choice of a university professor appealed to me for a few good reasons. I believed that the job would pay decently, but much more so because one would have more time to oneself for scholarly pursuits and constant reading. Generally, a university would require a professor to teach roughly from eight to ten hours a week, as one would need to spend more time on research, looking for new things, to keep constant the interest of the students, while preparing for lessons and so on. Hence, I thought that a job which would give me the freedom to utilise my time as I please and study what I desired should be the ultimate objective. The quantity of holidays was also an important element to consider, as I have been since long a travel lover. My parents would always point out that if I had been saving the money I had spent on music and travels, I would have been a rich man.

On the other hand, becoming a diplomat, at that time, seemed like a long stretch, mostly because acquiring the job meant getting through a selective process, which I believe was really quite a nepotistic one as well, then. I felt, therefore, that there were not enough equal chances as we have now. For that reason, although I really did want it, my inner self did not feel convinced about reaching that goal. Some inner voice would always prevent my thinking from going that way, as if pushing me to dismiss the whole idea altogether.

That being said, I have never really consciously had any big ambitions about my future. It felt more like they somehow would come to me naturally. Considering all the things I have achieved in my life, I never strove towards any of them with the intention of reaching a certain place. What I did, and continue to do, to this day, is that whenever I am presented with any undertaking, regardless of its nature, I strongly believe that my duty is to give the best of myself to it, at least to my knowledge. It is imperative for me to stay focused on the task that is right in front of me, give what is required at that moment, rather than look ahead with an ulterior motive. This way of thinking has always helped me to be content with what I have.

As I made my way into adulthood in that manner, at the age of twenty-four, when I was at the University for Post-Graduate studies, heading towards becoming a teacher, I received another blessing from God. This was in the form of a choice I had to make, between teaching at my university in Fes or joining the Ministry of Foreign Affairs (MFA) as a young diplomat, after successfully passing all the steps of selection.

Indeed, after I had gotten my Bachelor's degree in English Literature, I was granted a postgraduate studies scholarship, which I was happy to gain, at the prestigious Sidi Mohamed Ben Abdellah University in the historical city of Fes. Known to be the spiritual and cultural capital of Morocco, this emblematic city houses, also, according to UNESCO, the oldest still functioning university in the world, Al-Qarawiyine. As part of the training for a would-be professor there, and while I was preparing to eventually become a Medieval English Drama teacher at the same university, the scholarship also allowed me to give a handful of lectures on behalf of my professors, as their assistant, mainly during their absence.

Incidentally, it was just then that the competitive exams for a position in the Ministry of Foreign Affairs and Cooperation commenced and were made accessible for the potentially qualified candidates. I remember during that time, the former Foreign Minister, who also served for more than one term as Prime Minister, Mr Abdellatif Filali, advocated against the preferential system that had existed in the functioning of the Ministry. He was opposed to the idea of employing only those coming from prestigious or influential families. Should there be times when a person had failed to do the job required of them, it would become slightly difficult to reprimand them because of their connections and influence in society. Therefore, he wished to make this exam less exclusive and give equal opportunity to everyone to compete for the position, to seek excellence, in the hope of assembling a more sincerely committed and dedicated workforce.

Subsequently, the day of the examination arrived, and I believe more than 4,000 candidates turned up for the exam. As it happened, I had been selected after clearing both the written test and the interview. However, at the same time, I was offered and assured a permanent teaching job at the university after completion of my post-graduate degree.

It was amidst this entire flurry that I had to make a decision that would change my entire life and would last throughout the rest of it. Furthermore, I felt God was generous and had blessed me abundantly, as did my parents and family. The only two professions I had set my mind on, since I was a young boy, came to me both at the same time, and it was entirely up to me to choose from! I was very delighted over this good luck of mine, but equally distressed and in a serious dilemma over having to choose one over the other. I had deeply desired both for a long time. In building my arguments and as a remedy, I devised them, within myself, according to gains and losses, strengths and weaknesses, the objective being to make sure that whatever decision I was to take would be the right one.

As I contemplated on remaining at the university, all things considered, I realised that, at a point, it seemed to me a slightly monotonous job in the sense that, even if I were to evolve and change as a person, the job would somehow remain the same and I would be required to perform in an almost repetitive, albeit evolving, manner. Alternatively, the Foreign Office was a completely new thing to me, and in that aspect, I felt there would be more challenges to take on. I was instantly drawn to the latter and decided not to turn down any opportunity to try out something new, somehow mysterious, and challenging.

As a matter of fact, even my desire to be a Professor of English Literature was a decision I had made before knowing a single word in English. In school, as we moved higher in our studies, the students had to choose between Arts and Sciences, almost like a specialisation. I had a fairly adequate grasp on both the disciplines, but was really more inclined towards choosing Languages and Arts, as opposed to Mathematics and scientific subjects, which I used not to favour or find pleasant. I told myself that I would go ahead with the former, and in that first schooling year itself, I decided I would make English the primary language in whatever career I would ultimately choose. Even with having missed out on the path I did not take, somehow everything aligned perfectly as the things I learnt from there helped me a great deal on the path I had to choose eventually.

After I had made my decision and proceeded with the necessary arrangements to move on towards what lay ahead of me, the Head of the English Department at the university, Mr Bentahila, was quite cross with me for choosing to leave the university, after six years of studies, including the two post graduate specialisation years. He was unhappy that their prospect of having someone they had been preparing for a long time, and who would teach a subject in which it was slightly difficult to find good professors, came crashing down with the news of my departure. However, I must tell you that I almost lost the job as a diplomat because communications at that time were not as fast and easy as they are now, and I used to get the information about the results almost in extremis.

Indeed, I remember that I visited, during a working day, a close family, whose house I was using as my permanent postal address, when the shop owner near them told me that there was a postman who had brought a telex to deliver to me. But since I was not there, he took it back to the main post office, asking the person to inform me as soon as possible since it was of utmost urgency. He could say no further, and I did not know from where, or from whom, the telex had come in my name. I was perplexed, even scared somehow, and wondered what news that telex could contain. Besides, it was past six o'clock in the evening and the post office had closed for the day. Hence, I had to rush to the main post office to implore the night duty officer there and to request him to permit me to read the telex meant for me.

It was a rainy winter night, and entry inside the post office was not allowed after six p.m., except through an aperture, a sort of counter. When I enquired of the officer about the telex sent to me, he took a little time. Then, with a big smile on his face, he invited me to get closer to the gate of the office. He told me it is an official communication from the Ministry, without adding another word. He, too, was into sharing the joy, while my heartbeats were getting quicker at the thought that the results of the written examination for entry into the Foreign Service may be in that paper. He knew the content, but I hadn't... yet. Though my smile did not revive, he shed a relaxing spell, which made me forget the cold night and my earlier worries. While handing over the piece of paper in an envelope, Mr Said (the name of the duty officer), knowing that I wouldn't be reading it comfortably outside because of the rain, invited me to step in and read it effortlessly. The telex paper did not have more than two lines. After putting in the name and full address, it read, 'You successfully passed the written examination at the Ministry of Foreign Affairs and Cooperation. You are invited for the oral assessment… which would take place no later than the next day, at 10 o'clock, in the headquarters of the Ministry'.

It was almost seven in the evening, when I received that sizable piece of information. Somehow, another kind of fear took over, and that was: Would I be able to get to Rabat on time for my oral exam? I knew that I wouldn't be given a new chance if I had missed that one. Therefore, as I was focusing on how to get there on time, another more complicated dilemma was hindering my state of sobriety. How would I dress up? I didn't own a tie at that time, as I was not in need of one, as a student. Because the Ministry itself is a formal space, I knew that dressing up properly, with a tie, was almost as important as the exam itself. I remember my ultimate choice was to look as smart as possible, even if I was without a tie. Thus, a white-and-khaki striped shirt, which made it look a little elegant, teamed with a nice jacket I used to wear, mostly while interacting with the students, was my final decision.

With the issue of the dress partly resolved, the next and more important step was what means of transport would allow me to be there on time, as it was already beyond nine o'clock in the evening by then. So, after taking what I needed, I headed to the railway station to catch any train that would take me to Rabat. Fortunately, I discovered that there was a train, which would arrive at Fes Train Station, slightly beyond eleven, coming from the north-east direction. It was an old train and I wondered how many hours it would take, and in what state I would reach Rabat. The journey would last for a good portion of the night. At that time, there were no double rail tracks on this route, which meant that one train would have to pass before the lane was cleared for the next train. Somehow, this minor inconvenience did not disturb me, apart from the impatience to reach Rabat. Deep inside me, I was also hoping to stay on the train as long as I could, on a rainy and cold night!

WHAT IF... WHY NOT?

Once in Rabat, I spent the remainder of the night in the train station as I didn't want to disturb any family member, so early in the morning. To cut matters short, I was at the Ministry at least half an hour before the scheduled time.

At the Ministry, to my great relief, I looked conveniently and even better dressed in comparison to many of the other people convened for the interview ahead. Inside the room with the examiners for the interview, I remember one of them telling me that in the translation I had had to carry out, from Arabic to English, during the written exam, I had made a serious mistake. The subject matter of the translation was a letter sent by His Majesty the King to the Prime Minister at that time concerning the new "Investment Charter", and I had mistaken the word "investment" for "investigation". I believe this oversight was because of the fatigue I felt after the gruelling seven hours spent that same day in the earlier subjects. The examiners had stated: 'We liked your translation despite this terrible error and we want to dig deeper and let you prove your knowledge, especially in the English language.' I told them that I, too, had realised my mistake the moment I had come out of the examination centre. But since it was to their liking, it had pushed them to consider it as an involuntary mistake. I appreciated their gesture and thanked them for giving me a new opportunity to prove my fairly good level of Shakespeare's mother tongue.

The exam took longer than the normal slot dedicated to each interviewee. I didn't feel time while interacting with the five examiners, each taking me to a different direction, and the questions were asked in three languages, Arabic, French and of course English, the focus being naturally on the latter, keeping in mind the mistake I had made earlier, in the written exam. To be honest, I was generally satisfied with my performance, and I could see that in their faces also, as they were exchanging pleasantries, and pulling my leg now and then. I believe they were also testing how my reactions would be accordingly and how broad and open-minded I would be. However, having gauged their motive, I remained calm, as one would never be sure of the outcome of such deliberations.

On returning to Fes, I carried on with my normal life, waiting for the final results, which took a long time. Meanwhile, I visited my sister Aisha, two years younger than me, who was living with her husband and his parents in a city called Taza, three hundred kilometres away from Fes and about five hundred from Rabat. I would constantly ask here and there if there was any news about the results. When my sister also enquired about them, soon after my arrival there, I decided to call the Ministry directly and seek any clarification on this matter. Nobody wanted to inform me about the results, and the switchboard operator was passing the phone from one person to another. Finally, there was a person who had remarked that he had seen on the list of successful candidates the name "Maliki", but couldn't decide if it was me or somebody else, as he couldn't remember the full name.

So, I had, once again, to take the train, the same day of my arrival at Taza, and rush back to Rabat to check the final results, as the newcomers had to be there to confirm their acceptance of the job, and nobody could tell me the deadline. I wondered if it was not already too late. During the train journey, the problem of dress came looming large again. Once in the capital, I took a taxi and asked the driver to take me to the Ministry headquarters at Roosevelt Avenue, without delay. There, I found that the list of successful candidates was posted on a board, and my name was among the lucky selectees, to my great joy and relief. I was thrilled at the idea of being part of this prestigious Ministry, and more importantly, there was still time to confirm acceptance of the job.

There were more than seventy candidates who successfully passed the exam; it was the first-ever large number of entrants at the level of the Ministry. I clearly remember that my number on the list was fourteen. Later on, I learnt that the list was put up according to merit. Internally, there was one more hurdle to overcome... the University position. But I had no time to dally as it was the last day of acceptance for the Ministry. I decided then and there to avail of the chance, reasoning that if I had to withdraw my decision later or retract, it would be possible. However, the reverse wouldn't have worked anyway.

The official joining date was 27th November, 1989. The irony of the whole affair was that I had to live again in the same small house in Rabat, where I had lived while I was still a young boy of eleven, in my secondary school. But this time I would be living there, mainly for the first few months until I find a house to rent in the neighbouring area, with a new perspective. I had, indeed, lived in it during my junior school years as a pupil on the brink of failure. Now I was back in the same place after having been successfully accepted into the Foreign Service. It seemed to me as if I had gone out of Rabat in those early school years by a small door and had re-entered the house, once again, through a larger gate as a triumphant young man. It was with a feeling of shame that I had left the family home the previous time, and today, I was returning to it like a knight warrior in shining armour! The occupant of the house was different this time, a younger cousin, Abdelkrim, who was a journalist at the National Press Agency, the *Maghreb Arab Press*.

At work, one of the incidents in the early days was when a distant relative from my mother's side informed me that the Chief of Protocol in the Ministry had selected me to be among the officers of his division. 'Do you want to join this Division?' he had queried. My answer to him was: 'I don't know what "protocol" means in this context. All I want is to learn the job, and I don't mind from which position or division in the Ministry I would start.' I was posted, finally, at the Directorate General of International Cooperation, which incidentally was closer to my house than the Ministry Headquarters, where the Protocol Division was located. Thus, on 27th November, more than 40 newcomers like myself were received by the Human Resources Department Head in that big building of twelve stories, in the heart of the capital, Rabat.

This time, I was rigged out in a brand new grey suit and a tie to make a proper entrance into the Ministry and my new professional life. I also told the Chief: 'Can I ask you for something, sir?' He answered nervously in front of the others, 'This is your fresh posting in the Ministry. How can you dare to ask something on your first day at the job?' Without giving him more time to continue in that mood, I interrupted him and said, 'Please don't misunderstand me. I want to be posted to a tough division, where I can learn on the job quickly.' The Chief was taken aback and said, 'Well, I've never met somebody who wants to be very hard on himself from the start; but no worries, you will be served, my boy.'

My assignment was in the Technical Cooperation Division under the supervision of Mr Mohamed Benomar, who, by the way, became my Ambassador in Cameroon. Initially, there were thirteen of us to be attached to his Division, but after two weeks, he requested seven from our group to look for another assignment as they were not fit enough by his standards! My work with him was very tense; a very good learning experience with diversified tasks. In fact, I got along so well with him that he had decided to take me as his Deputy for his next posting as Ambassador of His Majesty the King of Morocco anywhere. In this perspective, he was a tough teacher. Fortunately, I was a studious learner and complied with his requirements and lived up to his expectations. As the official ceremony by the King took longer than was expected, so did my posting abroad because I had promised to accompany him. In fact, there could not have been a better boss, humanly, professionally, and socially speaking.

In looking back on these incidents and the way I got the job, I would simply give a piece of advice, though I may not be in a position to do so: don't force destiny: your destiny will come to you! My entry into the service had reinforced in me, and seriously, this conviction, because, at its face value, I was almost nonchalant and the job had almost slipped through my fingers. Yet, I would be asked to react almost in extremis to redress or, rather, even more accurately, follow my destined path. How naïve I had been! What I was doing was what my destiny was pulling me to do, towards the path traced for me and that, one shouldn't oppose… I didn't, and I couldn't.

CHAPTER 9

THE IMPORTANT AND THE ESSENTIAL

In the vast and huge world that we live in, with over eight billion unique individuals, each contributing to an ineffable diversity, there is but one indisputable truth that affects us all in the same manner: regardless of who we are, what we have or don't, the ultimate reality for every single one of us is death. In essence, we are all moving towards an assured destiny; what happens between our coming and leaving is another story. The only thing we claim to control, in this perplexing design, is what we make of the interlude between our births and deaths, between dawn and twilight.

Within that inevitability, one certainty that makes the fleeting nature of life less sombre, and surely adds nuance to it, is the promise of uncertainty itself, that will transpire in the course of events. In that regard, there is a saying that I've always found to be timeless in both its implication and effect: 'The past belongs to the past; the present belongs to us, and the future belongs to God'. It is the uttermost truth that wherever we go, what is gone is gone forever; what lies ahead can never be perceived until it is so; and all we are left with, to do as we please, is the 'now'. We live for the present, *we are the present.*

None of us has any knowledge of how long we have to live, or, for that matter, cannot even know with certainty what will come up in the next few hours. Thus, our time on Earth may vary greatly for each of us. Regardless of the length of our lives, the time we are given is never enough; our time is short and insignificant compared to the infinity of the universe. Hence, while we are collectively heading towards a particular end, the most important thing to be mindful of, I believe, is to live a little more happily and meaningfully as we traverse this remarkable path that the *divine power* has paved for us.

Of course, there are challenges in achieving such a life. After all, it is clear to see that at a time like this, the momentum with which life is moving by, is too quick, and it only seems to accelerate as one grows older. When you are a child, you look at your parents and the elders around you, and wonder how it must feel to be that old and think to yourself about all the time you have, until you reach their age. It seems like an eternity until then. Yet, within no time, you find yourself at 50, as if all that time you had, somehow, just vanished as quickly as you assumed the age of your parents. And even so, you still go on to think that old age is a good distance away from you, despite having had the opportunity to realise that time is catching up with you already; it certainly is.

Here, the truth is that we have all become so absorbed with what is happening around us that we forget to live life as it is; we forget to count our blessings as we go on and forget to enjoy all the small moments, and eventually lose sight of the things that matter to us.

Subsequently, it becomes exceedingly hard to maintain equilibrium between the *important* and the *essential*, or the fundamentals of life. This is by far the most distressing ramification of being heedlessly immersed in the whirlwind of life's hasty stride—even more so because in contemporary times, the notion of what is important and what is essential has become quite intermingled, when actually, it is not.

I think the two elements are being seen to belong to the same category, while we'd better consider and take into account the difference between them. Of course, we need to look at them through each individual's perspective and according to one's priorities, which are, at every point in time, never static. Generally, people tend to conflate the two and overlook the fact that what is essential is always important, and yet not every important thing is essential.

In my personal experience, these two concepts of the essential and the important have struck me as an element of my consciousness. At the start of my career, the essential things at that time for me were to marry a beautiful wife, have enough money for a decent living with adequate leeway for my hobbies, a fancy car… But on achieving all this within hardly a few years of my professional life, it looked a fairly short journey to materialise all these things. Also, I ruminated over the fact that the Almighty had been so generous towards me. He had endowed me with all these *important* things in a relatively short span of time during my career, in the sense that I had got married, acquired the necessary material things, and achieved suitable diplomatic appointments, after hardly a decade in the service.

But while looking back over time, and decoding these achievements, so to speak, it now seems that these things were too legitimate and reasonable, in their given nature, to be counted as aspirations. Then, there was still that urge to strive for other things since we, as human beings, are never satiated. From a very early age, we are always running after something; money when one is young, a house when a little older, fame or a good status and then, why not a yacht? The expectations, which can be exceedingly ambitious, keep mounting.

It was at this stage that I realised that contentment is a very good blessing and a wish to pray for to the Almighty to bestow on us. It is essential not to regret the bygone things, to value what we have at the present, as the past remains in the past and the future is in the hands of God. Also, in pursuing limitless ambitions, which can be a mirage at times, we forget to appreciate the things we have in hand, in the course of this constant and endless pursuit. Instead of being happy, we become constantly miserable in this race inherent to mankind only, among all others.

Over time, regrettably, the *important* has become more prevalent as the focal point of all humanity's endeavours as compared to the *essential*, which I believe stimulates a subtle growth of the existing pandemonium we witness in our society today. At the same time, I think, the ability to differentiate between the two, to begin with, has widely seen a decrease with time, leading to a growing trend in prioritising the *important over* the *essential*. However, one cannot deny the fact that the *essential* things encompass the *important* ones, that everything that is *essential* to us is very *important*, while every important matter may not necessarily be essential. For many people, including myself, a clear distinction between the two lies in our list of priorities.

As everyone can speak only for themselves in terms of classification, the important things, for me at this point of time would include my career, my colleagues, my lifestyle, the numerous travels, whether it is work-related or otherwise, in a manner of speaking, the things you may skip or change at any point of time, yet they are not frivolities of life, as such, and the list can go on.

On the other hand, certainly, my family and our presence around each other, my children's education, our and my mother's health and wellbeing, along with those of my larger family, true friends, to name a few, pertain to the *essential* things. At the same time, I am sure the priorities of a young unmarried person, who is still in the phase of building a career for himself or herself, would differ slightly, if not definitely, as opposed to a married man and a father with children, two daughters, as in my case. The *essential* things basically could be the personal responsibilities that we have towards ourselves, our loved ones and ultimately our society, all evolving with time as we go through life.

In this regard, I would like to confess that, while pursuing my career, I have not been present in my daughters' lives in their growing process, as I should have, as a father. To resume it, though in a caricature manner, I would be sleeping when they left for school in the morning and when I returned at night from work, they would be, very often, in bed. In fulfilling that essential part of family life, I admit, I could, or rather should have, organised myself much better. I still wonder if that could have been possible. Perhaps I could have got up earlier or organised my official duties in a manner that I could be home earlier. In the bargain, I literally did not see my children growing up.

Hence, when my elder daughter, Ghita, announced that, after completing her high school, and after successfully passing her Baccalaureate exams, she had been accepted by the three French universities she had applied to, for medical studies, I was shocked and reminded of our reality in its most crude manner. My feelings at that time were that of bitterness and without thinking I said, 'But I didn't see you growing up!' I regretted having spent almost only weekends and holidays with the children, which were certainly, in terms of quantity and quality time, far from being enough, while it was my wife who was taking care of them as they were growing up. Fortunately, she was always there and fulfilling both my and her duties, relentlessly. I will always be indebted to her for being constantly present for them and educating them properly.

I also felt strongly that I had failed in that essential part of family life. I tried to find a softer word to describe it, but I couldn't. So my next thought was to try and keep her in Morocco instead of having my daughter live on her own, abroad. I was reminded of what my mother used to say, 'A guest is a guest even if he stays in winter, summer, and all the rest.' Her life in France, or elsewhere, would have been like that proverbial guest, and life would never be the same. Besides, it was a tendency in Europe, and still is, I believe, to always keep the best talents within their boundaries and make them stay there, after completing their graduate and postgraduate studies. Yet they would often be denied the normal rights a productive citizen should get in return. They are mostly, if not always and insistently, seen as outsiders and foreigners, for whom residence permits would always be facilitated due to their talents only.

The growing fear of the likelihood of losing her, for good, made me do all I could to keep her in her country for her medical studies. Besides, her being in a familiar and less stressful environment, she would be surrounded by her family. No wonder, I was literally, but discreetly, lamenting over this news and felt that God had blessed me by giving me a chance to "re-buy" myself, to literally translate an Arabic expression. I can't describe how happy I was at the thought of her staying with us longer in Morocco.

I remember having used the argument of the fear of failing the family and thereby losing them forever, two years earlier to my posting as Envoy to India and while Ghita was still in high school, when I had put forward my case officially before my then Minister,

Dr Saâd Eddinel El Otmani, adding that only a posting abroad could hopefully help me correct, even slightly, the neglect of my responsibilities as a householder as it would allow me spend more time with them. He was receptive and looked positive, especially with the numerous years I had spent in the Ministry. However, even if I could see that he was sympathetic with me and sensitive to the argument I presented, he said, like his predecessor, that it was difficult to accept it at that time, as "I was still needed in Rabat". Something I have never understood, except for probably their preference to remain in their comfort zone, as long as possible. However, isn't it true that we have always been taught that *no* one is indispensable? I still believe *no one* is; nor should be.

Indeed, my counterpoint was that it was probably a sign of an unorganised institution when a person is thought to be so indispensable that there is no available alternative, while in reality, there is and there has always been. As a consequence, there are only a few individuals who keep on doing the job, only because the hierarchy prefers to remain in the comfort zone by keeping them. We therefore don't realise that others miss the numerous opportunities which are normally theirs. The result was my own self-realisation in this matter. It was only I, and certainly the likes of my colleagues, who were to blame for this impasse, especially since we had overlooked the elements of essentiality and importance in our personal lives. I felt I should have set aside time for my children. The important thing for me was my job, but the essential was my family. The equation looks simple at face value, yet it is very complex.

I don't mean to imply that one carries more value than the other because both of these elements are integral in making a life whole. Yet, there are moments in our lives when we are faced with the challenge to find a balance between something that is important and something that is essential. Finding a middle ground where we are able to give the right amount of focus on both is not an easy task. More often than not, it is taxing and challenging, but surely, it cannot be entirely impossible. In the end, nothing really is.

I feel, nevertheless, blessed in this regard as my family has always been very supportive and understanding, although in their case, they may not have had a choice. From my personal experience, I can say I have faced and continue to face those challenges with regard to my job and my personal life. A person's job undoubtedly has a share in defining her or his priorities. The more one advances in age with the accumulation of experiences, and the further one progresses in their career, one's needs and classifications readjust along with those changes, and thus we make certain alterations to our already existing list of priorities.

As a diplomat, to reach the position of an ambassador is certainly a prestigious and gratifying one, as it is the crowning of one's career and by the grace of God, I have come this far. But it also comes with its own set of gruelling challenges and responsibilities, which are highly demanding in terms of energy and time consumption. After having reached all the way there, at a certain point, I realised how a great deal of my life had passed me by, that a lot had changed since the start and that despite having secured a certain level of comfort for myself and my family, it was hard to be in a position to always enjoy them.

On a different level, being too relentlessly caught up in the pursuit of a particular prospect in some way sends all the things changing around one into a state of oblivion. Indeed, as a bachelor, for instance, this part did not bother me as much. Before bearing the responsibility for all that I am now, in terms of family or otherwise, I lived life fearlessly. I found myself incapable of experiencing fear of any kind, to the point where it became a slight cause of concern when I realised it around an incident in Cameroon, to which I have dedicated a full chapter. However, once one begins to shoulder responsibilities, everything that concerns one affects those relying on him or her directly, regardless of the security and assurance that comes from being at the helm of affairs.

When I was a young diplomat, not long after I had joined the Ministry of Foreign Affairs and was just at the beginning of my career, my goals were simple. My expectations were limited; neither were they exceedingly ambitious, as I have mentioned earlier. I pictured myself content with a quaint little house, sharing my life with a loved one and having just enough to get by, which I earnestly worked towards, while my career was being built slowly, but surely.

As it turns out, after achieving what I had set out to do, there came the next phase, of what lies beyond attaining something we have set our intentions on. At some point, considering all their differences, from the person we have grown into, we start to develop a new set of objectives to achieve as we move ahead, having realised that there isn't really any point in limiting our ambitions. The ability of a human being to be satiated subsides gradually as we go further in our pursuits. Each accomplished task sets us off towards building another pillar for the new horizon we are looking to, and another gets added on, and another, and another. This may carry on until we reach the pinnacle of our career, all of which comes naturally without, in fact, much effort if we have enough faith and put in the necessary effort.

I remain unceasingly grateful for all that I have been blessed with in my life… right from the start: it spreads out from having caring parents, to being surrounded by all my loving siblings, and continuously being able to provide my family with the best that I can. However, as I strive to do the needful, my close family is deprived of having the comfort of my permanent, or at least, necessary presence at home, as a son, a husband, and a father. On the other hand, besides being an extremely time-consuming job, the work of a diplomat is also demanding in terms of energy, acquiring skills, office presence, public relations, entertaining a busy social life, frequent and unplanned travels, etc.

What is the rarely seen and understood aspect of my job, despite all the glamour it comes with, is what goes on behind the scenes. Beneath all the benefits and those visible privileges, there remains a persistent amount of pressure with the level of responsibility that we shoulder, the aftermath of which is endured by our social and personal lives. If I were to rectify my shortcomings with regard to my unavailability for my family flawlessly, it would mean that I would be required to readjust. I would cut back parts of the efforts I had put into the job, which, I can admit, have been excessive or needless at times, in order to enable me to provide more time for them and avoid the pains caused to the most loved ones.

Consequently, I would find myself compensating for my absence by making sure that I am able to provide my family with all their growing needs, which further requires dedicating more time to engagements with them as best as I can. Then again, more and more, and the vicious cycle goes on and on. This situation may not be set in stone, but this particular concern seldom escapes my thoughts in my search for the balance between the *important*, which here is my career, and the *essential*, which is my commitment and responsibility towards my family.

There may be neither a holistic understanding nor a precise answer to any of the above-mentioned complexities yet. There may never be. Life follows a dynamic pattern where change is the only constant. I believe that one of the most prudent approaches towards its unpredictability is to embrace its very essence and find harmony with, and in it. Through this and in the due course of my life, I have come to gain, no doubt, a clearer understanding of a very important detail. When we find ourselves in certain stages where we have to confront all the changes around us, nothing else helps better than going with the flow, as accepting all changes gracefully helps one respond to them in a better manner.

In realising that I have missed out on some things in the lives of not only my children and my wife, but certainly also my beloved mother, whilst striving towards being there for them in other ways, I feel a subtle wave of sadness. After all, there is nothing more fortifying to the soul than being in the close comfort of your loved ones. At a certain stage, you realise that after the point where most of their necessities have been fulfilled and you have done everything you could for them, there remains the question of what happens in the unforeseeable future when you may find yourself incapable of supporting them in the same manner. As a matter of fact, their needs may not remain the same either.

However, there is no more to it than that. We realise that, in retrospecting through the magnitude of all the things that have gone by, the past remains in the past, and the lived experiences should help us learn how to make our present delightful and rewarding. It helps us give meaning and sense to the things we do, as we move on. We have no way of knowing the future, and, if at all, the only way we can remotely come close to having a say in how our future is shaped is by being mindful of what we have now. This is why the present matters so very much. It surely does, and should.

It doesn't help to cry over spilt milk, and no amount of regret over what I missed out on in between will ever contribute positively to the making of a possibly better future. As of now, the best I can do for my children is to educate them correctly, orient them towards making the right decisions, enable them to be themselves, and not to oblige them to pursue a fixed set of paths. Above all, it is more important to be able to inculcate in their minds the ability to perceive everything for its value and not for its price.

Education for my children is an *essential* element at present, nurturing them in a way that they grow up to make positive contributions to society and overall, to humanity. When the day does come when I am no longer needed to do the same, I will find myself in a position to renew my priorities again, those which I have to pick up. I have no notion of how different or challenging the changes in my responsibilities might be in the future, but I surely hope to see them through purposefully, when I do get to that bridge.

It may be impractical to be in this constructive state of mind all the time, given that change also takes time. Nonetheless, to progress positively, it is necessary to reassess our priorities every once in a while, if and when we have to, regardless of whether the occasion presents itself or not.

Having said that, as things do not always remain the same, no wonder that something that we had felt was most important to us years ago might have taken a back seat in our present concerns, or maybe it has escalated. In either case, realigning ourselves is a conscious choice we have to make; change is an assured outcome with each event that facilitates it, but whether we grow along with it is something we should embrace heartily. In the end, isn't our life outlined by the choices we have made and those we still make?

As is usually the case, the delicate decision of veering towards responsibility in the light of the moment came onto my radar with my posting to Islamabad. This news was taken almost helplessly and even desperately by my mother. Of course, I had to give my consent to the posting, as declining to go to Islamabad, in the light of my dear mother's desires, would create a very poor opinion of me officially and probably affect my career.

This rat trap of a dilemma that surmounted my mind also made me realise how vulnerable and fragile our lives can be. I had no foolproof solution to decide whether I should be staying back in Morocco in deference to my mother's desires, or opt for pursuing my career in a manner that would benefit me. In short, I was on the edge of a proverbial abyss. The only saving grace that followed was the very few days' leave of absence from my official duties that I had managed to squeeze in this hectic routine, for making preparations for the ongoing trip and bidding goodbye to my mother, mainly, and siblings.

It was an emotional juncture for both Mother and me. She could not bring herself to let go of me and finally said, 'I can't stay at home with you going away. Take me to my brother's home where I shall stay for a while.' I knew that she was trying to lengthen the time she had with me while being driven to her brother's place. This feeling was confirmed when we had almost reached the place and were a mere two buildings away from her brother's place. She suddenly asked me to stop the car. She then sat with my sister on the stairs of the building next to my uncle's, and though she is not a person who is prone to displaying her emotions, I found her crying like a baby. I knew that the pain of the parting had overwhelmed her to an uncontrollable extent. May God forgive me for the malaise I had given my beloved mother!

For me, too, those tense moments were equally poignant. The sight of my mother in that condition was troubling enough. In addition, I, too, was tortured mentally, mulling over the recurring thought: What am I doing? To become an expatriate voluntarily and leave my dear mother in an emotional shatter certainly raised a host of cataclysmic queries in my mind.

Foremost among my ideas at that time was the question of existentialism which seemed to relay my angst as to the specific purpose of my life, my job, my mother, my family, and so many other interrelated questions. After all, I had been the individual who had taken the decisions that weighed me down at that moment and yet… could I have done otherwise?

These interpretative details of the preparations for the journey, and sundry matters, occupied my thought right through the journey to Pakistan. It made me a bit absent-minded outwardly as I just could not let go of the personal dilemma, as well as the emotional recall, in the company of my mother. Time and again, her spoken thoughts dogged my brain and obliterated all else. She had said: 'I feel as if your father has just died. So far, I have been bearing the loss of your father because you have been around and I had you, but with you leaving, I am now left without my main support.' My presence, which I had never realised till that moment, had been the scaffolding that had upheld her from breaking down at father's loss, and my leaving her was like the sudden collapse of her entire emotional support system. I was dumbfounded and wondered if that was a hint of rationality dawning, or a reinforcement of the nagging idea: 'You don't really have to do it!', I kept telling myself.

Even more distressing to me is that this life-changing incident unfortunately, cannot be singled out as a one-time occurrence. The tragic repetition of these feelings, of whether I was putting others to afflictions and emotional upheaval due to my decisions, surfaced yet again when I received my posting to India. This time, it was my wife who was more emotionally affected by the moment of leave-taking. She was almost on the verge of collapsing, even as the luggage had been loaded in the car, and we were saying our goodbyes to our daughter, who had to stay behind in Morocco and pursue her medical studies there. My mind furiously and blindingly debated the rightness of the decision I had made to leave her behind, and the heavy consequences of it, if not on myself this time but on my wife and my younger daughter Nada, too. It made me measure and quantify the worth of my decisions. Did I realise the suffering I had brought on my wife and children through my decision to further my career?

My mind was agog with a host of questions for which I had no clear-cut answers. In all this soul-searching and pain internalising, I was opined to philosophise on the difficulties of human existence, the ever-present dilemma of whether we are second to our job or not! Indeed, in the little cracks of my sobriety, there had peeped in a few traces of irrationality.

After all, our strong bonds as a nuclear family were the best shield we had. The depth of our values was strong and would not be whisked off the radar by a physical parting. Besides, as a parent, I am not in the habit of showing emotions outwardly, but the fact that I give them my all internally is imbibed silently and surely by them and in moments of estrangement. Yet, these links are never shaken.

My overriding motto, therefore, in balancing these troublesome trajectories that have influenced and also questioned my decisions occasionally, has been to try and rise to the level of the expectations of others, when and wherever I can. Here, too, it is the wise homilies of my dear father that I have tried to follow all through. He would often say: 'Mind the issues that can't be solved by money, for in their case you will have to make sacrifices to solve them. Money, on the other hand, can help compensate for some issues, not all, and certainly not always.' Time and again, in life matters, I have wholeheartedly tried to remember this piece of unshakeable wisdom.

Yet, I know, on the other hand, that every decision that has been made for us, every single choice we have ever made and even the ones we didn't make do certainly influence the course of our life and lead us exactly to where we are at present.

Chapter 10

Balance and Moderation

Growing up and becoming mature is a wide-angled vision for me. Hence, in the course of living, there is always the preponderant thought of what I should do and what I want to do. The dilemma has therefore posed a challenge not in terms of making a choice per se, but in trying to strike a balance between what I did and what I should have done. In fact, if I had the chance to relive my past and go back to my earlier days, I probably wouldn't have done things the way I did then. In short, I may have reacted to the situation while profiting from the hindsight of the accumulated experience.

The wisdom of this perceptiveness has also generated another angle of my observation, in that it has reiterated the fact that we, as individuals, are different from each other. We are not angels or demons, but simply ordinary beings. Humans. In life, there are moments when we don't look for takeaways... they simply come to us. It may be in the form of books that we lay our hands on, or persons who cross our paths in life, or moments that become etched in memory and these involuntary happenstances impact our life in the long term. Personally, I like to categorise such markers into a 'before' and 'after' phase, with marriage being at the middle ground, commonly dividing life into the phase prior to marriage and after wedlock. In the case of *yours sincerely*, the first phase, before 1995, is what I would mark as one during which I certainly had missed many moments and opportunities that I let slip by, due to a certain moment of weakness, one's education or simply nonchalance.

The post-marriage phase of my life is a time that drove home the veracity of marriage as a heavy-weight institution, bringing alongside the obligations and duties towards one's partner, as well as the centrality of sincerity and sharing. On the whole, my marriage made me realise that life was to be lived with a partner in all seriousness. Earlier, it was a much more fluid relationship with people. One could manoeuvre relations either by going forward with them or by taking a step backwards. In a trite confession, I would even go the length of saying that the latter behaviour was a way of weighing out people, or staying with people I found easier to connect with, or enjoying the atmosphere of company without social commitments.

But there were certain inbuilt safeguards within me that surfaced with an exercise in self-examination. I recognised that if an idea is ingrained in my mind, I would work towards getting to it, no matter how much time it may take to materialise. Thus, by applying the same principles in my social associations, I often reach my objective. This also happens when I put a person on my mental radar, for a good reason, of course. Yet, I concede, through my modest experience, that women in general are better at retaining their human associations, as they tend to compartmentalise them and would never really give up easily. In terms of behavioural comparison, women find it harder to forget a person who mattered a lot to them even after a long time. I believe many people would share that thought. Men, on the other hand, tend not to stick too much to such incidents as they are far from being as much persevering as their opposite gender.

Having bared my mental makeup regarding my take on human relationships, I should like to make it very clear that despite my love for human company, I am far from being manipulative in my ways and, even more precisely, my education has always denied me that. I generally veer away from using negative expressions about others and have tried to be authentic to the point of an overreach towards culling the perception of seeing things from the other person's point of view. These moments, when I have consciously or unconsciously tried to see things from the other person's perspective, have provided me with a feedback which I may repulse, or may treasure, or retain, for we are human beings with preferences, but also and generally share a common background, with social, cultural references and differences.

Human beings, I have concluded, are made both close and different. Thus, with some people, one can match one's persona, and the chemistry simply takes off. At other times, you don't always like what you get. You don't want to go with what you have, and yet, the obligations, such as one's job responsibilities or one's status, make greater demands at those moments, making choices tilt away from the personal to the proffered.

In this amalgam of the freedom to make choices as also the advancement in my life to a level of maturity, the twain have a common meeting ground linked to two striking occasions in my life. The first one was in the manner of a progression in which I felt grown up, in terms of my responsibilities regarding my relations with my younger siblings, as also my relations with my mother.

Though the two were somehow intermingled, the second instance was a direct and unmediated instance. It was linked with the passing away of my father, particularly the moments leading up to his death and the immediate aftermath of this sorrowful occasion. When this happened, we hadn't completed the construction of our own house, especially some last-minute finishing. We had shifted to this house for its larger area and also because the previous apartment we had been occupying was on rent. It is important to mention here that prior to my late father's illness, we had been living in relative luxury in government accommodation, occupying a sprawling government house, wherever we were, as he was a "*Caid*", a kind of prefect in charge of districts or localities called in Morocco "*kiyadats*". Sometimes these *kiyadats* can cover areas of thousands of square kilometres, especially in the south-east of Morocco, not far from the borders with neighbouring Algeria. But the change in circumstances, in the early 1990s, with his illness, was not as stressful as we thought it to be. This can be explained, maybe in the education we had, based on adapting easily to new situations. Our frequent shifting and changing places following my father's postings helped the family in readjusting, quickly.

What we had been blessed with is the realisation of the honesty of our father. As a *Caid* he was in a position where he could have made millions if he had wanted, and yet he had lived his life with scrupulous honesty, and more. What he remarked about his status is that he had left to his children a decent way of living, a good education for all of us and the reassurance of being able to walk with head held high with honour. He believed in the philosophy of teaching someone how to fish instead of giving them a day's catch of fish. As a big functionary, the influence of the image is there for all to see, but it is the "regard" that is important. In my life too, I do not care about what people would like to see and to that extent, I would not go out of my way to hoard unnecessary things, despite the pressure that the family could exercise on me at times. Instead of being content to stay in our decent apartment, the family could then push to move to a bigger house or bungalow, even if I had to ask for a bank loan to get it. Never.

Together with this level of maturity that dawned with my father's demise, what I like to surmise as "a little bit of common sense", is also one of cultivating a level of non-visibility in life, as being one of the inherited experiences from my father. Despite the social pressure and the culture in Morocco of acquiring as early as possible a house, what we would call in Arabic the "tomb of life", we learned from his approach to build, on priority, not a house of grandeur mounted with bricks and stones but rather a set of values to follow. I am happy that we live largely by these values, which still guide us in our relations. It is not always easy, mainly because of the growing importance of materialistic things and appearances over moral values.

These values also work as a philosophic reminder of inheriting the enviable legacy of being the children of an honest man. He had given us the very genuine values of good education, honesty and above all, the respect we should owe to others, regardless of their levels in society or circumstances that we hold dear in life, to date.

Of course, our life at home was not at all one of torturous austerity. There had been luxurious vacations to different parts of Morocco, such as to the seaside, and rides in decent cars. In other words, this amalgam of life's intrinsic values above trivia had resulted in our leading a simple, but happy life. So, when we had to move away from the government accommodation, to a new house, we had to sell the smaller house in Fes to procure land in Meknes and build a new one, surely much smaller than those we had been used to, but a comfortable home, where my two brothers still live with their children, along with our beloved mother. I had personally contributed towards its construction because at the time of building it, a little before my father's passing away, I was the only stable and permanent worker in the family who got money on a regular basis and who could, or rather should, lend a hand. My younger sisters, too, were there to be looked after, and I'm proud to say that they also received a good education and are today admirably fulfilling their role of motherhood.

But I am drawn back from these consequent developments to the immediacy of the night of my father's passing away in Meknes. At that time, I was happy to be back, the previous year, from my posting in Cameroon. I was living in Rabat, 140 kilometres away from the family home, and every fortnight I would pay a visit to my parents. Since the early nineties, my father had been living on dialysis, after the gradual failure of his kidneys. Therefore, he definitely was not at the top of his health as it was a rigorous four hour of being attached to a machine to clean the blood, and that, I believe, undoubtedly detered us from leading a normal life. And among family members, too, there was that subconscious element of cautiousness, when even one's smile was often kept at a level of containment.

During the ten years he was undergoing this artificial blood cleaning, one of my brothers would be the regular chaperone with him to the clinic, and after the dialysis session was over, he would drive back home himself mostly. But, as his health deteriorated suddenly this time, during the month of December 2001, his doctor, Mr Dkhissi, ordered that he should be kept back in the clinic under close observation. My brothers knew from the doctors that his vital organs were failing one after the other and his hours were counted.

All this was happening, without my being informed, as the eldest son, about the sudden deterioration of his health condition.

However, as if by premonition, when the phone rang at home around 11:45 p.m. that Thursday night, I felt my heart suddenly sink, and I instantly turned to my wife and said: 'My dad has died,' only to be told that I had no earthly reason to think so, especially since we had visited him the previous weekend and he was as usual… weak, but fine. She even chided me, saying that now I had begun to see myself as a person who could foresee the future! But then, I like to ponder over my mother's observation about me as she often says: 'You are special since your young age.' That night too, I felt something in my hair, even though personally I am no believer in such parapsychology. I still can't describe the feeling I had while the phone was ringing, but it certainly was a disastrous one, and that was the presentiment inside me. After all, nobody would call at such a time to chat, unless it is serious, or from dialling a wrong number. When I enquired of my brother at the other end of the telephonic connection, hoping he wouldn't confirm my worst fears, he informed me that though father was still breathing, it was his last moments, and I had better come urgently. It was around half past midnight when I drove to Meknes. Throughout the route, on the highway, I was almost absent-mindedly preoccupied with endless thoughts, but centred on one. Things would never be the same again. I was worried about my mother mainly, and my sisters.

When I reached home, the whole atmosphere around was a strange one. I knew that he had gone. Indeed, my father had passed away very early in the morning, on a Friday of the holy month of Ramadan, a very auspicious day which, in the Muslim custom, is regarded as the "best day of the week". It is also a propitious day, for if someone dies on that day, there would be hundreds of people praying, in big numbers in the mosque, and imploring God to forgive the departed soul as they would gather there for Friday prayers, and even more particularly, during Ramadan.

When I entered the room where his body was lying and kissed his forehead, I was struck by the smile I could see on his face. It was as if there was such a sense of relief from the suffering he had undergone for years, but, in particular, during the last few days. My thoughts turned to the belief, in the Islamic tradition, that falling sick, in the timeline of the disease, becomes a space provided to us to ask for forgiveness for our sins and be closer to God. It is thus a period of forgiving, and that beatific smile on my father's face at that time seemed to me to be a confirmation of this age-old idea. In fact, my brother-in-law, who too, had noticed father's smiling visage, enquired whether the doctor had actually confirmed his death.

Those paindful moments, between the time of our taking the body to the mosque and the interval when we were alone in his presence at home, were very difficult times for all of us, emotionally, especially for my mother and younger sisters. My brothers and I were busy preparing for the funeral and informing the family members. At the mosque, there were hundreds gathered to pay their respect to the departed soul, asking for forgiveness from the Almighty for him. It was a throbbing rhythm of humanity, and rippling through the crowd was the feeling that people like my father are those individuals who are classed as "rare". He was certainly a loved person and through his exemplary lifestyle, he had established such an impeccable aura of respect and love. Many of his friends continue to visit us till date, as a way of displaying their love and, through us, paying tribute to him, conveying their sympathy and not only displaying, but offering, their support to the whole family, in difficult moments, or on special occasions.

These experiences did not sink in immediately. As the eldest son of the family, I was caught up in the immediacy of managing the condolences pouring in, coordinating with my brothers, uncles and close family members for the funeral arrangements and the acknowledgements of the due respect that was being showered around. A strange hollowness engulfed my sensibilities as I went about the task of arranging the situational needs. I felt as if an umbrella shielding me from the harsh elements of life had been taken off suddenly, and I was left naked. There were newly added responsibilities to shoulder too, as my mother was now largely under my care, as also my unmarried sisters, especially since my brothers, as mentioned earlier, had not found their own way in life, yet. Even the legal material heritage to be up for division never crossed my mind. Besides, there was not much to divide. In fact, I had never had any intention to evoke it. I felt myself in a position where I had to reinforce the unity of the family and was not permitted the leeway of making a mistake. Thus, I took it upon myself to help my younger sisters not just through their school education, their needs, but also in the organisation of their weddings, later on.

Yet, there was no feeling of shouldering an unwanted burden that had been thrust on me. I was doing these things, not out of obligation, but out of conviction and, quite simply, I did them with pleasure. Hence, my prayers to the Almighty were not a call for help to get through the times. Rather, I made a plea to Him to give me what I needed, in order to meet, as much as I could, the needs of the family, provide as much help as I could so that they could live as close to the comfort they had been used to, as possible.

In fact, there have been moments when I am drawn into thinking that I was "baptised" into responsibility at an early age. Perhaps this had emanated from my being the firstborn in the family. Hence, I have been conditioned into an acceptance of my role with grace and have tried to be available whenever some important duty was required to be fulfilled, as regards the family. But there have been tectonic shifts that have shaken my dedicated resolve and exposed me to a state of vulnerability. This came mainly when the choice between fulfilling my responsibility and compromising it somewhat loomed uncomfortably before me. It also brought up the constant debate that has often dogged me... that between what is important and what is essential in our lives.

And again, that sixth sense of reflection kicked in as I thought to myself that when faced with a situation involving another person. I have never thought of taking advantage of the vulnerability of that person for in that case, I would have demeaned myself. It is a sort of pretentiousness that I will have stooped to. Whereas, if I convince myself to do the things that I consider right, even in terms of the job I am supposed to do, I would make it a point of self-examination. I then would ask myself: 'Are you satisfied with what you have done?' In short, I try as much as possible not to give importance to "negative elements" and tend to forget the wrongs people have done to me. My family thinks that I forgive a lot, but I can reach, also, a "no return" point at times, since it would then be hard, even impossible, to continue forgiving endlessly. As I said earlier, our relations should not be guided by material things and money. The value of things, my father always used to tell me since my early age, is always better than their prices. The former we cherish forever, and the latter we forget soon.

My personal responsibilities towards my children have largely been guided by the same principles. I try to keep them happy and have tried to provide them with a good education, but as for securing their future with hordes of inheritance, both financially and materially, I have alternative ideas. I do not fully succumb to the idea of living a life with the thought of endowing children beyond my means. I know that their education has cost me significantly, whereas the cost of my education was comparatively nothing, as we would hand down our books to our younger siblings, and only the notebooks had to be purchased for them. Thus, I believe in the philosophy of giving the best of life to my children, but with moderation.

At the same time, I cannot disregard the phenomenon of the conflict of the generations, which willy-nilly transfers some of its residue on the values that our children imbibe. It makes me recall an account that had been reported on the American billionaire, Rockefeller, pertaining to an incident which had transpired during the time when he and his son had gone to Las Vegas for a holiday or business trip. The senior Rockefeller had booked himself into a moderate four-star-like hotel, unlike his son, who had opted for the best accommodation in town. A perplexed journalist had posed the question of the differences in the choices of the father and the son, only to be told, by Rockefeller himself, that it was a question of individual values, 'He is the son of Rockefeller. I am not.' While in his case, the senior billionaire who built his empire through hard work could downsize in terms of financial matters, his son was in the privileged position of being upward, due to his inborn privilege of possessing a sizeable inheritance.

Likewise, in trying to provide the best that my status can permit, for my daughters, I have also made clear to them, through thought and deed, that circumstances in life are not watertight and are liable to change, and one must adapt, to advance. My children had been accustomed to the facility of travelling frequently in business class, and, even as a junior diplomat, I would travel most of the time, during my yearly leaves, almost exclusively in business class. This should not be seen as a sign of status, but because we have always had to carry a larger and heavier load of personal luggage, as we need to take so many things from home, particularly because of our unique Moroccan cuisine, which requires distinct ingredients. Also, travel agents too, are obliging to travellers with large baggage in tow, and would offer heavy discounts from their side, for long-distance flights, making the decision even more attractive for me.

On the other hand, when we were travelling on shorter holidays, we always chose to travel in economy class, and this point proved irritable to my elder daughter on a flight where it happened that our seats were not connected and we couldn't sit together in contiguous seats. Instead of giving her a piece of advice straightforwardly, I asked her to take a tissue paper near at hand and list down the privileges that she was enjoying and which were denied to billions around the world. The sobering aftermath was encouraging. I believe it was so because the realisation of intrinsic values and the fleeting nature of the ephemeral were brought home that moment for all of us as a family.

Chapter 11

Bandit Capers

It is always quite striking to see how some events remain carved vividly in your mind forever and affect your life, while others are wiped off and hardly remembered. As I retrospect over my early days and bygone years, I find myself recalling several things that had not crossed my mind during the last two decades, and even more. Some made me chuckle with certain realisations or got me shaking with laughter. Then, there are other moments that were overwhelming with emotion and brought me to tears—moments that have passed me by and left me with lessons and memories.

In recalling those instances, I have realised that nothing can prevent destiny. We move towards a predestined path. That is why I am a firm believer, and greatly encourage the good practice of helping others in need, with whatever is possible, and also emphasise the importance of being discreet in giving charity. Besides, it is believed that genuine charity, with full conviction, can help remove afflictions and misfortunes in our lives. It is proven that the more you extend and give a part of yourself, the more God will give back to you many times over. This thought has been the lodestar guiding my personal perception of life and underlining the importance of sharing the blessings and whatever largesse we may have been blessed with. On the other hand, prayer remains, for me, profoundly personal—and not just a ritual. It is, along with genuine charity, a way of giving oneself another chance to express gratitude, a natural recognition of the bounties that we have received so consistently throughout our lives.

Of course, I must admit that, through the course of life, my own priorities—like those of others—have changed. At first, it was the frivolities, you could imagine, and which haunt any youngster… a nice car, a nice house, many travels and, above all, a princess to marry, and certainly a good amount of money, enough, at least, to lead a comfortable life. But with the passage of time, my feet are more grounded and I now remind myself that nothing in this universe would go with me, and that I will return to my Maker, exactly as I had come, utterly naked.

Hence, I have always considered the things I have to share to be intrinsically simple in their truthfulness. Nevertheless, it is my hope that sharing a few of the experiences I've had—positive or negative—might help someone who may be looking to be entertained or in need of company, searching for guidance, and most of all, could offer a bit of comfort or upliftment in a period of disheartenment.

Ultimately, while this is about sharing my story, it dawned on me how much I was receiving from this experience, as well, from the moment I began putting my thoughts on paper. I have been exploring and rediscovering my own self, reassessing my own past through the lens of my current perspective. All the events that characterised my life—the decisions that shaped my future—I came to understand and apprehend them all, in a different light.

It is a journey within a journey. This inner quest I went on has been surprisingly gratifying. Even more so because I trust and hope that those around me, who persuaded me to share my experiences along this path and waited so patiently, feel just as much satisfied.

For this reason, it would be in the fitness of things that I share with my readers one of the earliest experiences that I encountered in my professional life, during my first posting abroad as a diplomat. This occasion is one of the two or three times that I was given a chance to live longer by the Almighty, and which has made me more philosophical and inclined to adopt a more analytical mindset. Thus, on being selected to join the prestigious Foreign Service in 1989, I started my career as a young officer in the Ministry of Foreign Affairs. After serving in the country for nearly five years, I was deployed in 1994 for service for the first time abroad as the First Secretary and Deputy Ambassador of His Majesty the King of Morocco to the Republic of Cameroon. The Ambassador was then Mr Mohamed Benomar, a wise man whom I had always considered my second father and mentor.

At the time that I moved there, Cameroon had been treading through an ongoing economic crisis. There had been a major currency devaluation that same year, further destabilising social conditions. Despite the little difficulties here and there, I can but admit that the six years I spent there remain deeply special to me and to my wife, who joined me later on. To this day, I value all the experiences I gathered over the years I lived there, having learned a lot with respect to my job, as well as some good friends I made over time, and everything that happened around, and in between.

Even after all this time, I can vividly recall the atmosphere of that evening. It was a rainy night, and the weather was exceptionally pleasant, despite the deafening thunder. I had an appointment with the Ambassador of Libya to Cameroon at the Hilton Hotel—the only five-star venue in town at the time. The appointment was scheduled on the eleventh floor of the building at the coffee shop, which also had a piano bar and a billiards facility. My guest of the evening, Ssi Ahmad, was elegant, middle-aged, and a former judge in his country. He was a political appointee, not a career diplomat.

It was like a theatrical setting on the hotel's top floor. The space where we were seated was the highest viewing point in the nearby area, and when lightning struck, the crackling streak of light made an unforgettable visual that is still imprinted in my memory. Then, there followed, after a while, the roaring thunders, heard even through the thick glass of the windows. In those days, the city was poorly lit, and in the enveloping darkness, the contrast of blackness against that striated line of light in the sky was both a pleasurable and memorable moment. All of us present there would be seated facing the large windows behind the bar area, stretched in a half-circle from both sides so as to fully enjoy the mesmerising view that would often make us speechless.

At this point, I would like to veer off from the moment in focus and place on record that Yaoundé, the capital where we were stationed, had the best weather conditions in the country, if not in all of the Central African region. It is located at about 800 metres above the sea level, so one did not need artificial heating or cooling, a rare phenomenon in Sub-Saharan African countries. It was also known as "the city of the seven hills", over which the houses, markets, and other buildings were scattered.

Back to our conversation atop the Hilton's highest floor, we realised that the lightning was losing its intensity although the rain continued to fall heavily with interruptions, now and then. That was how tropical rains functioned, easy coming and going, like horses galloping. When at home, you can hear the rain getting closer from a distance with a growing sound, since most, if not all of the roofs were made of tin.

We, thus, were ready to go back to our respective residences, when I extended an invitation to my host to join me for dinner at my place. It was the second day of Eid-al-Adha, the day of the *sacrifice*, wherein the idea of the feast is to offer mainly meat or money, or share something with relatives, friends, and neighbours. I argued that we could share the Moroccan famous *tagine* together and *kebabs*, which had been marinated earlier. Wasn't this precisely the occasion where sharing of the sacrificial meat is in accordance with the spirit of the day?

Fortunately, my guest accepted the invitation wholeheartedly and the *rendezvous* was made at home, after a while. Once there, we indulged in each other's company against the backdrop of the heavy rain that carried on into the night, even as we enjoyed a salubrious evening together over Moroccan mint tea, out in the veranda, after a copious dinner. The night went on until it was a little past midnight and time for him to go back home before it got too late.

As he was getting ready for departure and starting the car, I called out to the guard to open the gates. It was raining heavily, and the guard at the gate had taken shelter in the covered area at the side of the garage where the gate, hardly four meters away, would still be visible. His name was James, if I remember correctly.

As the house was on a promontory, we could easily see the gate of my residence. Hence, I had good control of the goings-on in that area, from the verandah. Also, since I was all alone in my sprawling residence, I had asked the driver of the Ambassador, Youssef, to stay with me in the house and keep me company until my family would come. There were enough rooms in the house. After dinner, he excused himself and said that he was retiring for the night, while we, protected from the mosquitoes outside with our well-netted verandah, had continued to enjoy the rest of the evening discussing and exchanging ideas and pleasantries.

In addition to the guard for my own residence, facing my house was the house of a former Home Minister, loaded with guards and our gates were barely eight meters apart. About 50 metres away was the residence of the Kingdom of Morocco, and the American Residence was hardly a hundred meters away, and above all, I was sharing the wall with my Embassy. Apart from the Unity Palace of the President, I think that the road we were all living on was unquestionably the most secure in town and well guarded.

Incidentally, I must explain on the side, a little about my guest of the evening, the Libyan Ambassador. Under the controversial leader, Muammar Gaddafi, Morocco and Libya, during the nineties, were not on good terms as Libya was supporting financially and militarily the Polisario—an armed group that unfoundedly claimed the southern provinces of Morocco, commonly known as the Sahara. But that didn't make a difference to our personal relations, even though such relations were not encouraged nor welcomed by our respective governments, especially if entertained by a diplomat. But my association that evening was entirely personal, and no politics were involved in our conversations. It was a celebration day where political differences didn't have room.

In the process of seeing off the Libyan Ambassador as he got into his car, I noticed that James, after opening the gate, was lying flat on the ground, face down. I had found that a bit odd and asked him if he was intoxicated. There was no response from James, except that his finger pointed elsewhere.

What followed, thereafter, was a strange, tense, chaotic, and complex couple of hours after our convivial evening. It became instantly apparent what was taking place. I noticed something move from my peripheral view, which I immediately realised were four legs. I turned and saw two strapped men emerge from the dark, pointing their guns at us, while closing silently the gates behind them. The younger bandit of the two said that this was a hold-up and that we should remain calm. I could guess that the agitated culprit himself would be around 25–26 years of age and could not converse in French—only in English—and later on, we suspected them to be from Liberia. We couldn't confirm this suspicion ever after.

In the middle of all this, I realised that they were robber-intruders who had been moving around the area and looking randomly for their prey or victims, especially since their chances were very low on a stormy night and in such a supposedly well-secured area. However, seeing us sitting in the veranda, they knew that at a certain time, the gate would have to be opened for my guest to depart—an undreamed-of opportunity to sneak inside unnoticed by the other guards, who were all behind their gates because of the heavy rain that night. In hindsight, I assume they must have lurked in the dark and waited for an opportunity to enter and attack, which was timed perfectly for them with the departure of my house guest. Despite being surrounded by all these places that are heavily guarded, the robbers had managed to penetrate through the security easily and unnoticed. We are never prudent enough, I concluded.

It is important to recall here that in those days, there had been a series of armed robberies, and it was known to almost everyone that whoever would be present at home during the burglary always wound up either dead or with serious injuries. It was also advisable to keep a good amount of money for the robbers, in case it happened, as they would be happy and less aggressive. In the middle of all this, I was momentarily surprised at how this could happen! I believed that the area where I was residing, Bastos, was one of the most secure places. I did not focus on this idea as the implication of this threat went far beyond the lives of those present on that night.

Now that the gate was closed easily and everything went smoothly as they wished it to be, the burglars ordered the three of us to keep silent, get down on our knees and put our hands on our heads. Then they enquired about who was the owner among us. 'I am,' I replied calmly, knowing that it was better for our safety not to mislead them. So, he asked me to usher him towards the reception area upstairs. While climbing the stairs, I was all the time reckoning that I could easily have kicked him off in a moment of distraction, especially since he didn't seem physically to be a strong man! But I could not. This frustrated me even more as any reckless move would endanger the Ambassador and James, who had a revolver pointed at them continuously.

In fact, not less than twice, I had the opportunity to strike a blow at my captor and leave him unconscious. The first time was when we were climbing the stairs, and the second time was when we reached the kitchen. I could have closed the door on his hand and left him writhing in pain. Both times, I was very close to doing so, and would have, if not for fear of how his fellow robber, who held my guest captive, might react to the commotion if heard upstairs. But what I was perplexed about was the absolute lack of any fear in me during the whole situation. Maybe I was tutoring myself with the idea that whatever would be would be, and we can't escape from our destiny.

Strangely, my calmness seemed to rattle the leader. He was nonplussed and blurted: 'You don't care if your life is at stake? I have never seen a "white man" not scared for his life, not showing any signs of fear. It seems you are not taking me seriously,' he shouted. As his anger mounted, he continued saying, 'I will shoot you in one of your legs to make you believe I am very serious, and my gun is loaded.' To which I responded, still calm, 'Which leg would you prefer to shoot—the left or the right one?' This reply only infuriated him further, much more so because it seemed that I was somehow gradually gaining the upper hand in the situation.

Somehow, at the back of my mind, I had reached the conclusion that even if something were to happen to my leg and I got hurt, everyone's lives would be saved, as by the time the trigger would have been pulled, the security would have been alarmed and would run to our rescue. Although that might have happened, I couldn't imagine the costs afterwards. I was much younger then, and the risks I took and the courage I felt that night were more reckless than calculated, I admit. I hadn't fully considered the consequences. But in that moment, I did whatever I felt right.

'Aren't you afraid of death?' he asked nervously. All that I found myself saying was, 'How can you shoot while you don't even know how to hold a gun properly?' I added serenely. 'You see, I don't mind death at all. If it should happen, it will happen. But it is a real pity to lose one's life in this way because of an irresponsible act of yours. The only thing that worries me is the sorrow of my parents', especially what my mother would go through if, God forbid, she learns about my assassination… Nothing more, nothing less.' I can't describe what a fright this thought gave me at that moment.

Despite this dreadful reflection, I added absentmindedly, 'For you it would be one more fired bullet, but for any one of us, it would mean a life lost.' Yet, while uttering those words, my voice grew louder and even more authoritative with a sentiment of real frustration and helplessness. Deep down, I knew any foolishness would be disastrous for all of us. In remembering those endless moments, I could see how irresponsible my reaction had been. It shouldn't have occurred; otherwise, I would have been responsible for any escalation or bloodshed. I was simply unable to conceive the gravity of the situation and what was at stake. In retrospect, I confess I was quite rash and impulsive, to say the least. Something was wrong with me that night, and I thought over it again and again. After this unbalanced conversation, the aggressor felt that I was gaining more ground and dominating him little by little, at least psychologically. He felt very uncomfortable. Then, he asked me to show him the other rooms to be able to identify mine so that they know where their focus should be.

Suddenly, he discovered by himself that Youssef, the driver, was in his room sleeping. As he woke him up abruptly, he noticed that he was keeping, as he always did, a big and long knife under his pillow. The side of its blade was shining each time it reflected light. The armed robber became very nervous and even looked scared for a moment. He then kept a reasonable distance from us. His trembling voice betrayed the fear that he was trying to conceal. He pulled himself together and resumed by saying that this was a hold-up and that we should, and needed to, remain obedient and calm. Immediately afterwards, he ordered his friend to come upstairs and join us in the reception area along with the Ambassador and the guard.

Now, we were all gathered in the reception area and were asked to lie down, eyes facing the ground. While the others complied, I refused, pretending that I had an asthmatic issue for a long time, for which I told them I was under medication and required to be sitting most of the time. Therefore, I couldn't afford to stay in that position for long, as I would lose my breath and suffocate! At that very moment, the younger guy sprayed tear gas on my face as he was visibly irritated with my behaviour since the beginning. While I felt very uncomfortable getting it straight into my eyes, it helped me consolidate my position as an asthmatic person who couldn't breathe. I can't describe how my eyes were burning, and yours sincerely's nose, too, as if it weren't enough already, had started running at that moment! Of course, this only irked them some more, although they complied by allowing me to keep sitting. The culprit was so confused by my reaction that he rushed to bring me water. My idea was to keep the conversation going and literally negotiate our safety first.

The other culprit went into my room to check how much money and how many valuables he could find. It would also allow him to identify the items they planned to take. After some time, as they were exchanging words in their own dialect, I could tell that they seemed happy. Apparently, they found more than they had expected. With the ongoing crisis in the country at the time, and the unpredictability of it all, more than ten banks had gone bankrupt, and it felt unsafe to keep money in any bank. Therefore, almost everyone had a good amount of cash with them, but much more so, for me at that point. That was the year I was to go back home soon to marry my fiancée, Karima, and it was not long before the big day was to arrive. I had started preparing for the occasion, however I could. It was no surprise that they found a large amount of cash as they were rummaging through my things and took all the pieces of jewellery—a bracelet and a necklace mainly—that I had bought for my new bride-to-be.

By the time they got to my closet, the leader and I had somehow been conversing affably. The robber genuinely started to seem like he was taking an interest in the things I had to say. As it carried on, he rummaged around my things and seeing a possible escape route, I began to help him with the choice of clothing he fancied while managing to put aside the things of value to me. Hence, I advised them that they would be of no use to either of them, for any reason, be it colour, size, or worn condition.

I could guess that they were concocting a plan to take the Ambassador with them to rob his residence subsequently and continue their burglary, as their appetite grew with the valuables they had found. I tried to convince them that the man in front of them was not an Ambassador but rather his driver, a fellow from Libya whom I had invited on Eid al-Adha to celebrate together. 'How would an Envoy of a country accept to come to the house of a simple officer at the Embassy?' They were checking his identity card and didn't seem to be convinced, initially, as the car that had been parked upfront proved otherwise.

However, I asserted that no Ambassador, considering his rank and status, would casually spend time with a junior diplomat, adding that the poor driver would be in serious trouble as his boss didn't know he was using the official car without his consent. This seemed to change their minds enough not to carry on with their alternate plan for that particular night. I had by all means tried to avoid their taking him as hostage and a security pass to his residence. Many armed guards were posted there. Besides, he had a big, ferocious dog. I was sure that gunfire would start as soon as they would reach there and the Ambassador would be in the middle of all the fired bullets from both sides. His life would be for sure at stake and could be easily lost, even if unintentionally. It would have been a serious, dramatic, and tragic collateral consequence. I was relieved that their idea of taking him was finally dismissed.

Meanwhile, the Libyan Ambassador was baffled and scared at the same time to find that I appeared remarkably calm towards our captors. I do remember him repeating and reciting endlessly "Ayat Al-Kursi" from the Holy Qu'ran, imploring and praying to God to save our lives. After that, having gathered almost everything they could find of value, the robbers plotted their escape and had come up with the idea to shoot our legs to prevent us from following them or, eventually, raising the alarm. Before they got to it, I persuaded them to take the keys, lock us in one of the rooms, instead, and leave the key wherever they liked. Once again, they reluctantly complied, although they looked very suspicious. Visibly, they were quite happy with their hunt. Somehow, I was, too, as this prevented any escalation and made them somewhat more amenable.

They eventually locked us all in my bedroom and hastened to leave as I made a big noise inside the room as soon as the door was locked. I suspected they feared I had a gun hidden inside and would follow them quickly. So, neither did we waste any time to call for rescue from the window, nor did we keep silent as we promised them, as we caused a huge commotion inside immediately. Alas! By the time help had arrived, they must have gone too far and no need to mention that they had along with them the Ambassador's car! Even my lovely musical keyboard, which I had recently received as a marriage gift from my Saudi friends, was no longer there, to my big disappointment. I had to order the same one later on. It was a special instrument because it had Arabic quarter notes in addition to the normal Western notes of the piano keys, allowing the player a wider range of instrumentation.

Within this milieu, I did a quick check of my personal losses. Besides the keyboard and a good amount of foreign hard currency, jewellery, and clothes, there was also a large wallet of different coins and banknotes, which I used to collect as a hobby from the different countries I had visited. Though they were not of much value in terms of financial exchange, the robbers made off with them anyway. Many of the coins were no longer in circulation, and thus, they were mere travel souvenirs, yet they still held value for a collector of coins. The whole episode left me with no taste for coin collecting thereafter. Fortunately, the Ambassador had not suffered much financial loss. Even his costly Rolex watch, which he used to wear on most occasions, had been left back home, and he was carrying only a few thousands of the local currency, the Franc CFA. Almost an hour after the burglars had left, the police arrived and the investigation and questioning continued until past four o'clock in the morning.

I lost no time in reporting the incident in the morning to my Ministry, as well as to my Ambassador, who was on holiday, back in Morocco. Knowing the reality on the ground, he was very understanding of the whole affair, but not the officials at the Ministry. Instead of making enquiries about my welfare and sundry details, those officials had pinned their sights and concentrated solely on what the Libyan Ambassador was doing with the Chargé d'Affaires ad interim of Morocco that evening in his home. Needless to remind here, as mentioned earlier, our relations with the country had not been too congenial at that point in time, and thus, my guest's relations had raised eyebrows back home, and enquiries.

But my Ambassador stood firm in my defence. He emphasised that the Ambassador was a personal friend and asked why the whole matter could not be looked at from a personal friendship point of view. This incident soon reached a natural and happy end, but its implications left their mark on me. I had seen the unpleasant side—and another face—of the administration and how it was often ungrateful, I thought at that time. Instead of taking things at face value and placing the interests of its staff at the centre of concern, I would argue, it tended to probe for hidden meanings and implications, even where none existed.

However, overall, I was quite relieved that no one's life had been taken that night; everyone remained safe. At a much later date, we retrieved the Ambassador's car from the neighbouring country of Gabon. We received information from our Embassy there, as we had reached out in the process of investigating the robbery. We managed to stop the sale of the car in time. That was the only thing we could retrieve from everything that had been taken that particular night. I used to joke with the Libyan Ambassador by telling him: 'Your official car was robbed from my home and our Embassy in Gabon brought it back to you. What more would you want?' This teasing went on for some time.

A few days after that incident, I was called to the police station to check if anyone among the arrested suspects was the culprit. When the Police Commissioner welcomed me into his office and asked me for identification of the people, I was completely outraged by the entire arrangement there. The scenario was arranged in a way whereby the culprits would identify me instead of the contrary. There was no protective one-way mirror, as is the custom, between me and them, and all the recently imprisoned criminals or suspected ones were brought to me at the office, where I was sitting, to look at them, one by one. Each one stared at me and would always recall who I was, in case they were identified. I said none of the culprits were there, and honestly, even if there had been, I would not have identified him. If I had done, I would have simply put my safety at stake. So, I refused to attend any identification session afterwards. I knew I would not get back what I had lost, but it was more important to preserve my safety and, even more, that of the others.

After this incident, word had reached the American Embassy that we had managed to escape an encounter with armed robbers within my residence. As a result, I was invited to their subsequent Crisis Management Seminar to share my experience with them and explain how I had managed to defuse the situation. I suppose I understood why they asked me to do this, given that especially then, it was extremely unusual, virtually impossible, to come out of such encounters unscathed, let alone alive. At the seminar, I remember what I told the participants about the incident. I candidly shared what and how things had happened on that night and expressed my hope that what I was about to tell them would help them somehow. I don't know if it really did, because I believe each situation is unique and the reaction cannot be foreseen by any means, though I can't deny it was a life lesson for me. I added that I had been reckless and only luck—and the will of God—stood by us that night. Our time had not come yet. It was as simple and blunt as that.

In all my life, I had never thought that a skill I had acquired at my job would also help me save lives one day. The robbers were satisfied with the amount of wealth they had looted, unaware of how I had been negotiating with them the entire time, for more than two hours, building arguments while they were under my roof. I did tell them, during the seminar, to always keep a fairly good amount of money in hand with them in case of any unforeseen attack, as it could help defuse tension. I added that *death* could come very easily and abruptly under such situations. For the burglars, it is just a trigger and one less bullet from their gun, but for us, it would mean a life that may be lost with it. I couldn't say more, as there was nothing more to say. That, by all means, is fate.

Later on, as I recalled the details of the event, I deliberated on how I felt and responded to whatever threat was present before us at that moment, and I was just as confused as the Libyan Ambassador that night. I realised that I felt no sense of fear. It took me back to my boyhood days when, as a young child, I was fearless to a fault—more so than any of my younger siblings. It was only after this incident, on the night when our mortality clearly lurked in the balance, as we were at the mercy of the armed robbers, and between the hands of God, that I began to understand the magnitude of my reckless valour. I do believe that just as God has bestowed every emotion in a human, so has the courage been vested in us. However, so as not to let unrestrained courage lead to any adverse development, we feel fear, and thus, it exists as a healthy and essential regulator. It should never be dismissed, nor should courage override it. After all, isn't ensuring a balance in all aspects of life that ultimately keeps us alive, safe and healthy?

Chapter 12

When There is a Will...

The path the *divine* has laid out for each one of us remains invisible to the human eye. Within this world, the winds of change that blow past us may seem turbulent at times. However, they often guide us towards our predestined direction. Regardless of how strange or chaotic these directions may be, I believe everything happens in its own time, in its own due course, with a reason and for a certain purpose.

Incidentally, there is no more to it than that, as I have always wanted to stress: the past remains in the past, to help us learn how to make our present valuable and rewarding, while retrospecting on the magnitude of all the things, in their absolute value, as we move on. Whether we realise it or not, every moment we live through is a connecting corridor to what is to come next. There is a correlation within the intricate structure of life that trickles into all the components enclosed within it. This truth became clearer to me at a point in my career in the mid-nineties.

This was on the occasion of the Summit of the Organisation of the African Unity (OAU), a grouping which had been set up for the purpose of coordinating policy and promoting independence and unity among the peoples of the African nations. My country, as a founding member of this Pan-African Organisation, its involvement in the matter requires a little background information. Although Morocco was a founding member of the OAU when it was set up in 1963, it had to withdraw its membership from the organisation when it admitted, without any legal background, the Polisario front, a separatist movement, created by Algeria and Libya, as a member under what their creator would like to call the 'saharawi Arab democratic republic–sadr.'

The attempt of the aforesaid creators of this project, was meant to prevent the completion of the territorial integrity of the Kingdom of Morocco, which incidentally is the only remaining North African country with a constitutional Monarchy system, a strong ally of the Western block, led by the United States, in opposition to most of the other republics of the region, except for Tunisia. These were closer to the Eastern block, led then by the Soviet Union, during the Cold War. This unjustified and unacceptable move led to Morocco's protest and withdrawal from the organisation (OAU) in 1984.

In 1996, the 32nd Summit of the OAU was taking place in Yaoundé, Cameroon. Officially, Morocco could not take part in the conference as it was no longer a member, while the new entity, sadr, was invited, as if it had been an independent country, along with all the other member States. This entity doesn't have, in fact, any of the prerequisites to become a country. As a sign of protest, in any country where such summits were organised, Morocco used to declare that the Ambassador of His Majesty the King, accredited to that country, would be on leave during the event and the *Chargé d'Affaires* would assume charge of the Embassy throughout the period. As the Deputy Head of Mission, I had to assume the heavy responsibility of leading the Mission and ensuring the follow-up of the proceedings and informing my Ambassador and consequently, my Capital accordingly. Thus, when the scheduled meeting of the Organisation of African Unity, the predecessor of the current African Union (launched in 2002), was taking place in Cameroon, my position, despite remaining under the guidance of the Ambassador, became extremely unique. It provided indeed the litmus test of my diplomatic skills, on account of a series of pre-emptive steps I would have to manage to pull through.

Once again, I must go back in time and bring forth the trying conditions that Cameroon had been facing just prior to this event.

The country had faced currency devaluation, and most banks faced reserve shortages, as a percentage of deposits and large levels of unutilised liquidity were withdrawn by customers, who lost trust in the banking system there. In fact, more than ten banks went into bankruptcy. Once a rich economy, the country was now undergoing a dark patch and difficult times, with a loss of jobs and rising crime. Therefore, the idea of holding the Summit of the OAU seemed to be an opportunity for Cameroon to turn things around and open a new page. Hence, large amounts were being given to refurbish the capital city and upgrade the infrastructure of Yaoundé for the upcoming important continental event. Security was reinforced seriously to prevent any problems for the visiting high-level delegations during the event.

Our house in Cameroon was a cosy one and not necessarily a lavish display. Small and bordering our Embassy, it was an independent house, surrounded by a modest lawn with a few fruit trees. It merely consisted of an unused ground level and a floor above ground level. The reception room of the house had a large space to receive a good number of people. However, the ground floor was left empty to keep the unused furniture, or that which was purchased to be transported home to Rabat when my tenure would be over. A while after we moved there, a table tennis was set up in the ground floor reception area, used for leisure time and games with friends. It also gave me an alternate space for meeting people in a cosy manner, instead of having it all the time at the Embassy. It also served for discussing anything with close lovers of the game, including a few officials of the Cameroonian administration. So, a number of high official friends from the State Protocol, the Ministry of Foreign Affairs, and that of Defence used to find it an extremely congenial moment and a good combination between exercising and having a drink of their choice. Indeed, my Ambassador and I enjoyed very close and courteous ties with the officials of the host country, Cameroon, at various levels. This good habit of having a table tennis facility at home, stayed with me since then and in the other postings, both in Islamabad and Delhi, where I currently have one as well.

When it comes to the summit, I didn't have crystal clear instructions as to what I was supposed to do. Nevertheless, it seemed to me that the main objective during the event, at that stage, was to convince the organising country to give the least exposure and visibility to the leader of the separatist movement known as 'The Polisario Front'—then Mohamed Abdelaziz, a Moroccan citizen, who had done all his studies in Morocco, but who was indoctrinated and manipulated by Algeria and Libya to lead his separatist movement against his own country. It is to be mentioned, also, that Algeria had closed its Embassy in Cameroon a few years earlier, much before my posting there. However, it reopened a few months prior to the summit to facilitate the arrival of not only the Algerian delegation, but also that of the Polisario. The latter would not have existed without the support of all kinds, including financially, mainly from Libya initially, diplomatically and logistically, from Algeria.

Therefore, when I spoke with my friends about the upcoming important conference, I was sharing my concerns about the welcoming ceremony, as we had reached a level where no subject was taboo amongst us. The fact that Cameroon had never recognised this entity as an independent state helped me greatly, in the sense that this was the official position of the country under which my friends would accommodate our wishes more comfortably.

Indeed, the so-called "SADR" was invited by the OAU as it was a "member", and Cameroon couldn't oppose this as it was the host of the event only. Nevertheless, as the organising country, its officials could decide on a few protocol matters, such as on meetings to be held, and on documents to be presented to the member states before adoption. So I requested their cooperation in all these matters. The most urgent thing, to my mind, at that time, was to give the least visibility in the media for the leader of The Polisario Front. My friends agreed on the principle, though they were not aware of how to do it, as there is a state protocol to follow for the heads of delegation in such events.

After exchanging views, we agreed at our level that the protocol would be reduced to the bare minimum to avoid media exposure. That would consist, I suggested, of sending a Protocol Officer to receive him at the airport and escort him to his residence, no more, no less! We all got to know earlier that he would be coming either from France or Belgium, but most probably from Paris. However, this reduced kind of protocol arrangement needed validation from the higher authorities, which we managed to get easily, thanks to our connections. To our surprise, but much to my disgruntlement, the Algerian Embassy got to know about our manoeuvres and altered the initial travel plans of the Polisario leader accordingly. Indeed, they made a few adjustments to the flight details to allow Abdelaziz to embark on the same flight which would be transporting the then-Secretary General of the United Nations, Dr Boutros Boutros Gali.

This sudden change of the flight details added to the difficulty of the whole operation. So, there was a little bit of disappointment, with the Chief of Protocol informing me about this new development and the difficulty they faced in adapting, mainly in terms of protocol arrangements. In other words, how could they welcome both at the same time but give the importance to the UN Secretary General, while implementing a lower level of courtesy for the other person when both were flying on the same flight and in first class? Despite measuring the complexity of executing this intricate "plot", there was never a question, for me, to abandon the whole idea.

After deep thought, I had come up with a diabolic plan which I shared with my Ambassador. He was shocked to hear it and very much doubtful about its applicability, given the circumstances and the limit of tolerance that our friends from Cameroon would be able to accomodate. Nevertheless, I asked him for permission to share the proposal and check with my friends at the Ministry of Foreign Affairs, while keeping him off the radar. I said to myself, 'What can't be achieved thoroughly can't be abandoned completely.' So, while I was playing a game of table tennis with an important high official, I remarked nonchalantly, and by way of testing the waters, 'What if we arrange two separate welcoming protocol proceedings for these two people, by reducing it to almost nought, for Abdelaziz, and organising an appropriate protocol welcome for Dr Boutros Ghali?'

I still remember him laughing his lungs out at hearing this and telling me, 'Are you serious, Mohamed? You must be crazy even to think that way.'

'I may be, but isn't it worth a try? What if I tell you how?' He realised how determined and serious I was about my proposal.

My interlocutor told me, 'It is a big thing. It surely is. So we shouldn't be messing it up completely. Besides, it needs a bigger and higher validation.'

All I needed now was to set up a feasible scenario which could be implemented without raising any suspicion, questions or, more importantly, creating any embarrassment for our friendly host country. I defended my suggestion to reduce protocol by reminding him that Cameroon had never recognised this entity, and that it was not obliged to organise a proper welcome for its representative.

So, the next morning, I went to the Ministry of Foreign Affairs as the matter consumed my thoughts so completely, and I had not stopped thinking all night of the details of the plan I would share with them. The idea I proposed consisted of keeping the media outside the aerobridge. Only the Chief of Protocol and another officer would be allowed to access the plane. Then, while the former would welcome Dr Ghali and engage in conversation with him for some time inside the plane, the other Protocol Officer would rush to greet Abdelaziz and give him the impression that he was "more important" as "Head of State". As such, the "plan" was to usher him out of the carrier as if on a priority basis. The idea was to inflate his pride and remove any doubts about the cunning plot he may have had initially in his mind.

The agenda, if validated, would be to welcome him first, quickly escort him through the service exit, with a car waiting for him below. It would be crucial to explain to him that they were doing it only for security reasons. The second step would be to close the door to allow access for the media to come near the aerobridge and turn on their cameras. The Chief of Protocol would accompany the Secretary General of the United Nations with full honours towards the VIP Lounge for the official ceremonial proceedings. My friends at the protocol of the Ministry found it a very hot potato to manage, but promised me that they would check with the State Protocol if it could be doable.

Meanwhile, I had done my homework with the higher officials at the State Protocol and the Ministry, sensitising them to be more flexible and try to accommodate the request of the friendly country, Morocco, as much as possible, for the reasons I had stated above. My Ambassador, Mr Mohamed Benomar, was a little bit concerned, thinking, though for a good reason, that I was abusing the kindness and generosity of my friends. Somehow, his comments made me uncomfortable, and made me conscious, even scared, that I may have done something which might have affected our bilateral relations. But, deep in my mind, I was somehow quite confident of the feasibility of my plan with a bit of chance and cooperation from the Cameroonian side. I admit, however, that there was discomfort and I was restless as long as the acceptance of the plan by the higher authorities had not come.

At D-1, I was pleasantly surprised that a friend of mine from the State Protocol reassured me by saying, 'You're right. Our relations with Morocco are beyond any consideration,' adding that an authorised official in the country instructed them to ensure our comfort. He said it while understanding the discomfort and even the embarrassment this situation might generate or put them in. And that was that!

To our satisfaction, everything went exactly the way it was planned, right down to the biggest surprise of my Ambassador and even the executing officers of this scheme. So, when Abdelaziz was taken through the exit door without any ceremony, he was resisting and threatening to raise it in the summit, arguing that the treatment he was being given was insulting and far below his expectations as a "Head of State". All the protocol and security personnel were ignoring his threats and defusing his anger by trying to ensure he was put quickly and smoothly, without further commotion, in the car. He was driven quickly to his hotel, away from the eyes of the media, which would have found the scheme a big scoop to report, had it come to the press and people's knowledge.

How relaxed and even triumphant I felt after I had received this report from my friends at the airport, to whom I conveyed our sincere thanks and appreciation for their precious cooperation, solicitude, and consideration. To my satisfaction and surprise, what followed was even more exhilarating. Indeed, during the same night, prior to the conference, I received a phone call at eleven in the night from a dear friend in the Department of International Organisations, at the Ministry of External Relations telling me that a big surprise was awaiting us in the conference without revealing what it was, despite my insistence.

Indeed, what happened the next day at the opening of the summit was beyond my expectations. On the table allocated to the so-called "sahrawi Arab democratic republic", the tag put in front of the seat of the head of delegation indicated "Polisario", instead of what they wanted their entity to be referred to as "sadr". This was a move which drove Mr Abdelaziz completely out of his senses. Outrageous, as you could expect, he requested that this serious error on the name plaque be corrected immediately. All the officials present there were presenting their apologies, saying: 'We are sorry, Mr President. It is certainly a mistake by a junior officer who doesn't know the gravity of the mistake he has made, and we assure you that the full name of your country will be prepared shortly.' The dramatic irony was that the organisers were fully aware of what was going on and what they were doing. Of course, the name was corrected, but not that morning; not in the afternoon; nor even in the next morning, but on the second and last day in the early afternoon, after all the media and the international press had taken photos of Abdelaziz as a figurehead of a separatist movement rather than a "Head of State", as he always considered and believed himself to be.

The cherry on the cake was that my friends created a process by which we were informed almost instantly of what the agenda for the discussions in the conference hall was. Indeed, my Ambassador used to receive by a police courier all documents that would contain something on the Moroccan Sahara before they were distributed in the conference room to the delegations present at the summit. So, we had to go through them very quickly and check if anything of prejudice to us was there, so that we could react immediately, mobilise the officials from both the host and the other friendly countries and ask them to lobby in our favour.

During the course of the conference, many complaints about the repetitive incidents were lodged by the delegations from Algeria and the Polisario to the Chairperson and to the Secretariat of the OAU. To their utter disappointment, Mr Abdelaziz was never received by the President of Cameroon, nor the Prime Minister, the Minister of Foreign Affairs or by any high-level official from the host country, despite the multiple requests and pledges made by the Algerian delegation in his favour. Both delegations were so unhappy that, hardly had the conference ended, when they took their flight back home altogether, on a chartered plane. It was clearly a manifestation of their frustration and, somehow, their disillusionment.

However, during the Senior Officials' meetings, the ministerial meetings, and then the summit, my Ambassador invited at various points, a good number of Ministers and members of different delegations, mainly from friendly countries, in order to exchange views with them, to gather their opinion on different issues, and as expected, to request them and thank them for their ongoing support of my country's position. Nevertheless, I could recall also that a few of our friends were critical at some points of the Moroccan foreign policy in Africa at that time, complaining mainly about the scarcity of high-level contacts and visits, and also the absence of more consistent cooperation, in a few particular fields. They also suggested that a few actions could be undertaken to make our rightful and just position heard louder.

As for the friendly gestures that the Cameroonian side extended at different levels for Morocco before and during the summit, I have never been able, of course, to thank them enough. I named all those high officials and friends who have made our *national issue* theirs, and for the amount of solidarity and cooperation we received from them, which I would never be able to repay, as so much of the risk they took was high. It was enormous, invaluable and priceless.

The importance of this incident in my career is the lesson it taught me, which I have put, since then, as a most cherished and magnificent moment in the glory of friendship, as a lasting treasure, in that it could produce miracles. Additionally, I also learned that I should never hesitate or lose trust when it comes to conviction in our cause and to the interest of my country, because the love of one's nation has always been a virtue that comes from faith and patriotism.

I can also confess that from that conference, the perception of my Ambassador towards me had changed for the better, but also his expectations from the small being that I am had grown.

So when the summit was over, I proposed to my Ambassador that the report prepared by the Embassy ought to convey the truth as we got it, however bitter it may be. I was honestly doubtful that my Ambassador would be bold enough to accept the narrative as it was built up. He also told me, 'I agree; we should tell the truth the way it is, and not write what people are pleased to read. Besides, I am hardly one year from my retirement. The worst thing that could happen is that my tenure would be terminated. But even then, I would put my head peacefully on the pillow and sleep, as my conscience would be clear.'

His attitude somehow solidified my trust in the system and in his authentic personality because many things used to go wrong, as the untold truth, in many cases, was not reported as it should have been. In fact, he strongly believed that by reporting meticulously the truth to His Majesty and to the capital, he would have provided a great service to the nation.

On receiving the report of the Embassy, long and detailed as it was, the then Minister of Foreign Affairs and Cooperation, Mr Abdellatif Filali, found himself in a serious dilemma, as we were told by his Office Chief. He was indeed torn between making a synopsis and losing the strength of it, or sending it verbatim as it was; a thing he had never done before. We were happy to know that the second option had the preponderance over the first one, despite a certain resistance from a few of his close collaborators.

During the few days after the report had been sent, the Ambassador and I were joking amongst ourselves that our recall messages ending our tenure in Cameroon would be wired any time. But to our satisfaction, a few days after the report was delivered to the Office of His Majesty the King, the then Ambassador Director General in-charge of Bilateral Cooperation, Mr. Maâti Jorio, called the Ambassador to convey the following message from our Minister, Mr Fillali:

'His Majesty, May God Preserve Him, has read the full report with great interest. He has asked me to convey to His Ambassador in Cameroon, His satisfaction over the clarity of the report and the truth it conveys.' The Minister reported further that His Majesty had added the following remark: 'I want people to tell me the truth as it is.'

The Minister also conveyed through the same channel his thanks and gratitude for the good work accomplished by the Embassy throughout the conference.

You can't imagine how relieved we were on hearing this feedback and evaluation from the *Highest Authority* of the country. That news was enough fodder to keep us happy for a few days. It further reinforced the conviction inside me that, wherever there is a will, there will always be a way. It all depends on how persevering we are towards our belief and the clarity of our objective.

This conference also showed that small things can make a difference; that history matters, friendship matters, belief in others matters, and that money can only help, but it surely can't always pave the path to success or glory. Above all, sincerity in friendship is far more valuable than any price you can put to measure it. Last but not least, modesty, I believe, remains an important clue to credibility in building relations and in sustaining true friendships. In short, as they say in India, "be zero to become a hero" or as my dear friend, Mr Ratan Tata, has always been believed to embody the adage that "money brings fame while modesty brings respect".

Now, with a bit of a distance, and building on the modest experiences that I have accumulated through the 35 years of my diplomatic career, I have come to the conclusion that a good diplomat is not merely someone who dresses well, or writes well, or speaks well and is fluent in many languages. All these are important indeed, and represent an indivisible component helping to fulfil one's duties. However, she or he should be, in fact, as much as they can, all these, but more importantly, she or he must be the person who can solve a crisis or a given situation at midnight, over the phone. In other words, the success of the mission of a diplomat depends largely on the level of their integration into the society of the host country. Its success would rely on the number of connections and friends they have made, at different levels, and who will be willing to pick up their calls at crazy and uncivilised hours, to offer help and go a step further for them on all occasions, without putting, definitely, at stake the interest of their own country.

Chapter 13

Deepening Diplomatic Skills

The start of the 1990s in my life was marked by a coincidence that led to the intertwining of the personal with the professional. Indeed, while on the one hand, there was a serious and enticing offer for a full year's training abroad, on the home front, this opportunity coincided with my father's illness worsening. He was barely 48 years of age when he suffered kidney failure. Due to his professional commitments, the family was living quite far from places with adequate medical facilities and treatment, which could have prevented him from reaching such a critical and irreversible state. Thus, he had ended up in a condition where his survival was completely dependent on dialysis, three times a week. It had resulted in a situation where we had to move to Meknes in the Centre-North of Morocco, to avail the facility of artificial, but regular, cleaning of his kidneys.

This shift, albeit providing the appropriate medical facilities, had affected the entire family in other ways. As a senior with an administrative position, we, the family members, had the comfort of residing in sprawling government houses. Now, we had to quickly find and adapt to a modest apartment and make the necessary adjustments towards a different and almost a new lifestyle.

On the professional front, as a newly recruited Foreign Service official, I had just received a good and opportune training offer in the year 1991, in Pakistan. I had been selected to join the Eleventh Specialised Course at the then Pakistan Foreign Service Training Institute (FSTI), which later on became the Foreign Service Academy, in Islamabad, along with a group of twelve other junior diplomats from various African countries and another from Maldives. Our batch also consisted of 13 newly recruited officers of the Pakistan Foreign Service, who had successfully passed their exam. As I had never been to any of the countries of South Asia till that time, this was not only an interesting experience, but also a rewarding selection. I thought it was to be my first contact not just with a subcontinent, but also it would also familiarise the participants, so I could get acquainted with the politics of the region.

Despite my father's deteriorating condition, both my parents, especially my noble mother, put aside personal feelings and encouraged me to take up the offer. 'What's there is there, and you can do nothing about it; you should build up your own career', was their reassuring consolation, and so I left for this maiden and almost one-year-long "posting" to Pakistan, feeling in a better frame of mind. Yet, somehow, it was not an easy decision to take. I also reasoned that in my absence, my mother would not be left totally helpless, as there were three other brothers living with her at that time, besides three unmarried sisters, who were still at home to help her in her hour of need.

My first two weeks in Pakistan were not without their attendant tribulations. Although the other members on the course were extremely congenial and I liked the professional opportunities the course offered, it was my stomach that was subject to nothing short of abject torture. As a partaker of an essentially Moroccan diet, naturally spicy but not hot, I was not used to so many chillies, in every form, including, at times, fruit desserts "adorned" with spices, known as "*chaat masala*". At first, I was determined to bear this minor cross like a martyr, but soon the results were becoming apparent. As my metabolism was not geared to such a diet, being far from what I was used to, the results were that I lost seven kilos of weight in three weeks, a feat which I would certainly be happy to achieve these days!

Finally, in sheer desperation, I called the chef in charge of the kitchen and told him of my difficulty. He at once took corrective steps, and the food turned palatable to a large extent. But what I discovered on the side was that I had not been the sole victim of this tribulation. Most of the other members from the African countries had been suffering similarly, but had preferred—for reasons I cannot quite understand—that Mohamed Maliki should be in the forefront and bell the cat, while they remained smug and undiscovered, on the sidelines!

As a diversion, it had struck me then, as now, that countries with predominantly hot weather have an appetite for spices and chillies more than countries with a cold climate. The Moroccan diet, which is notably rated among the top cuisines worldwide, is generally considered one of the best because it accommodates all tastes. Indeed, all people can adjust their dishes according to their tastes without altering the essence of the dish selected. In other words, Moroccan cuisine has a knack for blending the additives, without necessarily changing the core flavour.

Back in the classroom, I realised that I had cut a distinctive stature from among the foreign officers on the course, especially with the faculty at the institute, who were my instructors from the Pakistan Foreign Service. In fact, the former Foreign Secretary, listening to me speaking with him in English, was visibly taken aback, because he asked:

'Where did you learn your English, Mr Maliki?'

'I learnt it at the University of Fes in Morocco, Sir,' did I reply.

'Impossible, it can't be,' was his reaction while paying me a compliment, saying: 'You speak good literary English. Despite your Arabic-French bilingual background, your command over English is praiseworthy.'

While I felt truly flattered by his observation, I explained that our institution in Fes, from where I had graduated, was teaching us English in what they told us was "the received pronunciation"—the King's English. I did not know what difference that made, but I remember it was very strictly followed as we had to transcribe endless texts phonetically to make sure that we were equipped with the right rules of British English. He commented that he was surprised, but happy to learn that in my country, there was such a level of proficiency in a foreign language, like English. I also told him that I dabbled in poetry, exclusively for personal consumption, to strengthen my ability and command over the language. Alas, with the daily exercise of my profession, my literary English has reduced a lot and has become more oriented towards reinforcing my language skills in diplomacy.

During our continued conversation, I also elaborated on my country's educational traditions and explained that debates on Islam were held in traditional centres of learning and had produced eminent scholars throughout history. Besides, Morocco being an Islamic Arabic-Berber country, it was also known for not just one major city of scholars, but for four imperial multidisciplinary centres of great learning since ancient times, namely in Fes, Meknes, Marrakesh, and Rabat.

Surrounding areas around these cities had developed and also become important destinations for learning, including remote areas in the south and north of Morocco, particularly for Islamic studies.

Back to the layout of the course that I was attending in Pakistan, I must say that it was a prestigious opportunity for me. The faculty was made up of hands-on practitioners, as the staff was drawn from academia as well as the Pakistan Foreign Service, most of whom had been previous Ambassadors to several countries. Besides theoretical deliberations, we used to have close-to-reality based situational exercises which were of great importance as, in those days, Pakistan was facing the peak of the Afghan crisis, with the 1992 Peshawar Accords and the newly created Afghan leadership's keenness to build strong ties with the neighbours. These accords resulted in the proclamation of an Afghan Interim Government called the Islamic State of Afghanistan. Though most of the factions accepted them, there was reticence and opposition from other Islamic parties, including the Hezb-e-Islami, whose leader was no other than Ghulbuddin Hekmatyar. So, naturally, there was concern from Pakistan about the stability of the neighbouring country. The discussions on international relations were largely dominated by this passionate subject and the future of the region in light of these developments. It was a great learning experience for all of us.

Outside of the institution and the official routine, my days in Pakistan were synonymous with genuine welcoming gestures by the local population. I was invited very often to events at Pakistani homes, including wedding ceremonies and sharing *iftaars* during Ramadan. On such occasions, I was somewhat amused at the cultural differences at these celebrations. At Pakistani weddings, what struck me as unique, in a Muslim country, was the customary dowry by the parents of the bride in the sub-continent. This was quite in contrast to our custom of the groom being the gift giver rather than the recipient. Of course, the local custom, which originates from the Indian Sub-continent, was based on a sound logical base which argued that a bride could not possibly leave her parental home empty-handed when going to her in-laws for the first time.

And again, during Ramadan, when I was invited to the *iftaar* celebrations at the breaking of the fast, I found that the ladies at this occasion were in full make-up. This, too, appeared quizzical as Ramadan is a pious religious occasion and a spiritual thing where one concentrates the mind on the best way to present oneself before one's maker, rather than add to one's physical and outward attraction with external decorative touches. To my wife's query on this, much later, when I was posted there in 2003, our maid would argue that 'fasting is for God and we want to look our best during this sacred month for Him,' adding that 'the make-up was not done for the human eye to enjoy but for the glory of the Creator—seeking for blessing and forgiveness.'

Yet, if I were to choose what the uppermost experiences were during this training, without doubt, I would rank my travels to the various regions of Pakistan as among the most memorable. Right at the outset, I realised that each of the regions and cities within them had something special to offer to the visitor. Lahore, I found, was a bustling city and a foodie's delight despite the level of chillies there, while Karachi, a sleepless city, would give a fairly similar impression as Mumbai, with huge traffic and big noise. The unique experiences for me, therefore, were my visit to Balochistan, in the areas bordering Iran and Afghanistan. Also, the food of this region, in mountainous areas, and then colder than the plain and coastal cities, was a very palatable change, and I gorged myself on the varieties of *kebabs* and the various rice *pulaos* and breads. The chilli component was definitely more tolerable because the region's cuisine was influenced by Iranian, Afghan, and Central Asian food tendencies, due to the geographical proximity to these regions.

Of the lot, if I were to draw out a single memory from this travelogue, it would definitely be our visit to Quetta. What I recall was the fact that, though it was the winter season when we arrived, the weather was unusually hot. A local hearsay about the chances of an earthquake erupting when the weather experienced extreme heat proved to be a premonition, as this was exactly what happened, that same day, in the evening.

We were enjoying dinner at a four-star hotel in the city, in the company of the Governor and other important dignitaries, when suddenly, conversation came to a halt mid-sentence, as tables and what was spread on them began to move. The food was split all over. Soon, I noticed that the chandelier in the hall was shaking, and the lights went out. There was panic all around, people running everywhere to take shelter and shouting 'earthquake, earthquake!' Then, as the electricity was restored after a few minutes, and a semblance of normalcy returned, people began to recall the customary belief in those parts of an earthquake following within a few hours of freakish weather conditions that had just elapsed. In that moment of crisis, it seemed hard to dismiss this credence casually.

The extent of the damage was evident the next day, when we learnt that the epicentre of the quake had been a few kilometres away from where we were lodged. There was a huge crater in the ground in that spot, and we were told it descended to a few hundred metres below ground level! It was scary for most of us. My African colleagues were literally disturbed by the incident and became impatient, insisting on leaving the region and going back to Islamabad at the earliest, especially when they learnt that the aftershocks would come and could also be strong.

I thanked God for his endless blessings as I remained untouched, then, and for having survived not only this earthquake but also many events later on. That was my foremost thought at a trying moment such as this. The only plausible explanation I had always found was that my time hadn't come yet. As we rightly say, the utter truth is that there are many causes, but only one *death*. When it comes, it will come exactly when and where it should.

When the training was over and we received our certificates, it was hard to say goodbye to all the friends we had made and with whom we had literally spent most of the time together. We certainly departed with good memories and, somehow, in the course of our training as young diplomats, we had changed greatly from the individuals we were upon first arriving in Islamabad. I, personally, didn't leave soon after, as I decided to travel to Lahore, and from there I visited India, mainly the capital—New Delhi, Agra, and the region, for the first time in 1992. It was so different from what it is currently—less crowded and far less polluted. I have the feeling that it was a different era altogether.

Chapter 14

A Wish Becoming Reality

The Pakistan saga was now drawing to a close, as the duration of the course had run the length of its scheduled period. But in my mind, I was not prepared to take a direct plane and head back to Morocco at the end of the course, before trying to fulfil one of my earlier wishes and accomplishing a dream. Ever since my high school days, I had nursed three ambitions that I desired to fulfil during my life. Of course, they were all linked to travelling—my ever-irrepressible delight.

My three wishes were:

1. To see the Taj Mahal
2. To see the Great Wall of China
3. To cross the Congo River

It is quite common to have the ambition of seeing the wonders of the world one day, like the Taj Mahal and the Great Wall of China, but the Congo River left a very deep impact on me, as it stirred my imagination while I was in high school. Indeed, during our lessons on geography in my schooling time, everything seemed superlative about this river, and somehow exaggerated, at least to me. Being a person of South Moroccan origin, at the gate of the desert, water has always been seen as a blessing and a very precious gift from the Almighty, even to the extent of bordering on the *divine*. So, conceiving this huge amount of water was beyond my imagination. I was also wondering if we had this amount of water in my region, desertification would never present a permanent threat to the lives of people there. No doubt, my considering it as a wonder of the world was one of the ways of glorifying the might of God.

In 1992, the opportune moment arrived to fulfil the first of these three aspirations. At the closure of the course, I decided to travel to India. I planned to fly from Lahore to Delhi and, after a few days, head to Agra to visit the Taj Mahal, before going back to Pakistan to take my flight to Morocco.

What I didn't realise completely at that time was that visiting India after a stint at a foreign service training course in Pakistan was a diplomatic *faux pas*. In India, my moving around as a diplomat who had recently spent a year in Pakistan aroused suspicion, while on the Pakistani side, my move alerted the secret services into action mode and they deployed personnel to follow me and shadow me, wherever I went, during the whole trip, and perhaps even beyond.

My realisation that I was being closely followed struck me in a vicarious manner. As I had lodged myself in a well-established guest house in the capital, I found that there were some faces in the crowds becoming more and more familiar, which gave me the impression that I had seen them earlier, especially in the lobby area of the guest house. It was only when I returned back to Pakistan, after the visit, that I was told how the Inter Services Intelligence had followed in my tracks, and how my close Pakistani colleagues at the academy had gone through long and tough interrogations regarding our relations and about my movements. However, they ultimately had to give up, after having been convinced I had no political associations, intention or objective, apart from my love of travel and curiosity for discovery.

In these entire goings-on beneath the surface, the central focus of my trip, that of seeing the Taj Mahal, remained unaltered and as pristine as the building itself. As was customary among Agra travel organisers at that time, foreigners wishing to visit the wonderful monument of the Taj Mahal were extended the courtesy of being picked up by a representative of the travel agent and escorted around the site, so as to make the trip a memorable and smooth sailing one. Hence, as I was the first tourist to be picked up on the bus, before sunrise, I was given the front row and ringside seat on the bus from Delhi to Agra. I was seated right on the other side of the driver, a decidedly comfortable seat. It was a very premium place to enjoy the scenery, the road, and the villages we passed by.

Despite the panoramic view I was enjoying, the striking sun started to bring discomfort as my face was seriously hit by strong rays. I found myself requesting the tour guide to arrange, if possible, another seat, which would be located in a shadier spot. He came back in a few minutes to inform me that the bus was full except for one single vacant seat, next to a middle-aged lady in the centre of the carriage, in case I would agree to travel with a co-passenger alongside. Of course, I was, as the sun rays had started to have their effect, and I wanted to remain in the best shape, at least, for the whole day of this long-awaited visit. I had been awaiting this moment for so long that I wouldn't let it slip between my fingers, by any means.

It turned out that the mid-50s, my fellow passenger, Katherine, was a Canadian doctor, mother of two sons, and an inveterate traveller herself, who had been part of an official delegation that had visited Morocco three years earlier. They undertook that trip in the framework of the implementation of a socio-development programme financed by the Canadian International Development Agency, commonly known in French as ACDI. She had very pleasant memories of her visit, and when I asked her which city or place she considered her favourite choice, to my surprise, she mentioned Merzouga—in the far east of Morocco, at the gate of the desert. She elaborated that this visit had stood out in her memory because of the amazing sceneries, therapeutic benefits, and above all, the hospitality that had been extended to her and her team by the local *Caid* or Commissioner of the place, who had arranged a timetable of attractions for them, apart from their official meetings, including a programme of folk songs, music, and, of course, Morocco's "amazing food" as she liked to stress each time.

It so happened that she spoke warmly and extensively about the Commissioner—how nice he was to them and how attentively he had overseen their stay, and how generous was his hospitality. I was happy, somehow proud, but at the same time, intrigued and even a little curious to know more about the person she was describing, to remove my doubts.

Since my father had been posted as the Commissioner of the region of Taos, under which Merzouga fell administratively, the place she had mentioned earlier, I decided to probe a little further by asking subtly pointed questions, sufficiently tricky to the extent of irritating her and raising her apprehensions, of course unintentionally. Then, by a stroke of luck, I had a photograph of my father with me in my purse, which I was keeping during my travels. I held it up for her to survey, saying: 'By any chance, is this the gentleman you are talking about?'

She turned pale, literally speechless, as if she had seen a ghost, and her eyes were wide open. For a few seconds, she couldn't utter a single word, and I thought she was suffocating. Slowly, her face retrieved its colour and lit up with recognition as she exclaimed, 'Yes, it is this same gentleman who made our trip so memorable.' Then, it was my turn to be surprised, because I realised that it was he who had extended such hospitality to her delegation, not only as part of his official responsibility but also as part of his own nature.

She could not help but remark how small our world is and how it is memories of places that keep associations alive forever, within us. That is the idea behind federating our world through the good things in life. Of course, she had enquired after my father and was saddened to know that he had fallen sick, one year earlier, and was living on dialysis. We suddenly felt so close to each other as if we had been friends for a long time. I tremendously enjoyed the whole trip in her company, mainly while driving to and from Agra. Katherine was a joyous and really entertaining, experienced person, who was so agreeable to talk to and to learn from at the same time.

For me, too, this journey to Agra and seeing the Taj Mahal, its magnitude and detailed work had its own quota of unique takeaways. The bus ride with the lady had been informational, as well as self-reflective. My mind began to reflect on my father's life journey, a man who had started his professional life as a teacher of French, but had assumed another government responsibility as a simple administrator, and was climbing the ranks in the local administration, within the Ministry of Interior in Morocco. He had been shifted from teaching to the administration because of his French language knowledge, at that time, which was largely utilised besides Arabic, by the Moroccan administration, mainly, right after getting independence from the French protectorate, in

1956. Through his hard work, he made his way up till he became Commissioner—or what we call in Morocco, the *"Caid"*.

But in that moment of reflection, it was not only these factual details that resurfaced, but I recalled my father's lifelong habits, as well. The courtesy that he had been used to extending to everybody that he met, regardless of who they were, including the Canadian visitor with her delegation, was part of his generous nature to always give the best of himself whenever and wherever it was required, or when circumstances permitted. It was quite natural, almost an obligation for him, to project the authentic culture of hospitality of his region in the South and, by extension, of Morocco. He also used to offer a lot of charity, which he preferred to call "sharing what we have" with people whom he thought were most in need. I confess that we try to follow his path, but I am sure it is hard to equal him on this. It was his philosophy in life, and he was also very good at "splitting" his money on things he liked, such as travelling, movies, and changing cars.

Back to my trip to Agra, there was, then, my own set of takeaways. On reaching my chosen destination, the Taj Mahal, I was filled with emotions on seeing how the fifth Mughal Emperor, Shah Jahan, had glorified his deceased wife, Mumtaz Mahal, in those medieval times. The Taj Mahal, apart from being a magnificent structure and engineering marvel, stood elegantly, thus, as an embodiment of the place that women must have held in the high society of that time. As for its engineering highlights, I was impressed with the attention to detail, the carving, and the symmetrical arches in different directions. I was literally stupefied when the guide told us how the four outer pillars of the Taj, built between 1631 and 1648 by the chief architect, Ustad Ahmad Lahori, were slightly inclined outward so that they would fall away from the main building housing the tomb, in the event a strong earthquake or any other calamity.

WHAT IF... WHY NOT?

There was also the memorable moment when a local guide, on knowing I was coming from a Muslim country, Morocco, escorted me—assisted by a worker—to the room below, into the chamber housing the actual remains. Outwardly, it was a pristine, unadorned space, but it was impossible for me to overlook the sensitivity of the space. And when the guide had lit a torchlight, sticking it on the walls, the ruby-red flash emanating from the walls, reflected by the light, seemed to make it a chamber aglow with rubies. It was these understated statements of sensitivity, with which knowledge had been applied in the overall construction and embellishment of this beautiful monument, which has drawn me back to this site time and again. Yes, the wonder of this site remains a complete experience for me always, and I recommend it as a must-visit to every Moroccan delegate or visitor to India.

There were other, less ornamental, but equally memorable takeaways from this maiden landing on Indian soil. Strangely enough, it centred around cows that were seen in big numbers rambling about roads and even highways. In fact, our bus driver had to slow down, from time to time, on the way to Agra, and even had to stop in the middle of the road for one of them to exercise her right of way—while we waited patiently, till she had safely trotted to the other end of the highway. But the gem of the takeaway was when I spotted a man in torn and shabby clothes, carrying greens and herbs in a basket, in his hands, which he offered the animal to pick and choose and munch! It was quite visible that it was his own food, but he was thrilled that all the herbs and vegetables were taken by the cow. That was a cultural phenomenon nonpareil, I concluded then. I was also impressed by the respect people showed to animals, not only to cows but to the other species. India represents a safe haven to all of them, I am sure, including those which may represent a potential threat to travellers on the road and also to local people, at times.

Alongside this light-hearted remembrance, there were other recollections of the negative side too. The sight of so many night squatters sleeping on the sidewalks along the roads was unpleasant and shocking for me—a phenomenon which I don't see these days in that magnitude, fortunately. Yet, I also recall that the skies above the city those days were clear, a lot more blue, and the roads did not have so many cars plying on them. And wonder of wonders—there was so much gold adorning deities in temples, and yet nobody would dare touch them, despite India of that time being classified as a very poor and populous country.

It made for a compendium of the rational and the irrational—the predictable with the opposite. It ended up swelling my personal experiences, sharpening my insights, and tasking me to demonstrate an analytical temperament, while also understanding the essence of tolerance, accepting cultural differences with conviction and good humour. Needless to add, it left me with an overall very positive image of the country of Gandhi—India—to which I am honoured to be accredited, after completion of almost three decades of my diplomatic career... Something I could never have imagined at that time! I am happy that no one will have to worry about their future as it is, and our destiny will always remain veiled, but to God.

Chapter 15

The Softer Side of Diplomacy

When I was entering into an official matrimonial engagement with my wife, Karima, we didn't have any particular prerequisites vis-à-vis one another. I was already living in Cameroon as a junior diplomat, and all she needed was to bring with her her personal belongings. Nevertheless, I couldn't resist asking her mainly two things. First, I had asked her to get her driving licence ready, and the more difficult of the two, to accept giving up the idea of having a job. The former condition was important for her own mobility, and it would make our lives less stressful, as I intended to buy a car for her. While the second may sound very selfish on my part, I was convinced that it was the best choice, taking into account the fact that my own job was already demanding for both of us, and would necessitate frequent transfers from and to Morocco, as a career diplomat.

However, I made it my personal obligation to allocate a kind of a monthly allowance, the amount of which would be determined by my position, abroad or at home—the idea being to allow her a kind of monetary facility that would give her a certain flexibility, when it comes to her personal matters. I can't pretend that it can replace a job, but it is a way of recognising the sacrifices she has made since then, to make our life, as a united family, comfortable and more balanced. Her consent was even more crucial as we were hearing now and then of the problems that would emerge in the lives of couples when both work, especially if one of the spouses was a career diplomat.

Therefore, it was somehow like cutting off a potential problem that might emerge, at the root, by removing the very seed that may cause it in the future. After almost three decades of marriage, my daughters, Ghita, Nada, and I, feel blessed to have her in our lives. I am and will always be indebted for the sacrifices she has made, and still does, to fulfil her part in the obligations towards representing our country in the best manner, while being fully aware of the privilege and importance of belonging to an old nation with a great civilisation and a strong cultural heritage—namely, the Kingdom of Morocco. This has been of great significance and a source of immense pride since we got married, but it became even more important when I was appointed as the Ambassador of His Majesty the King to India in 2016. We both had apprehended the enormity of the responsibility placed on our shoulders and were ready to do as much as we could, what was required in order to live up to the expectations of the high authorities of my country, at various levels—and most importantly, His Majesty.

In fact, I would say with confidence that since I joined the Ministry of Foreign Affairs and Cooperation in 1991 as a diplomat, I, and later my spouse, have genuinely tried to reflect the generosity of my country towards our guests. While this may appear overall comprehensive enough, when it comes to a stage of representing my country as an Ambassador, the situation is distinctly unforgiving at this higher level, since there would be no leeway any more. The details would certainly have to be blemish-proof and suitably becoming, in order to fulfil my role adequately enough, at least to the best of my knowledge.

Therefore, whenever my wife and I welcome visitors and friends into our home at the Residence of the Kingdom of Morocco in Delhi, we keep in mind the grandeur of the country we represent and which we feel is an obligation to reflect and embody, while hosting our guests. Most of the time, I am pleasantly satisfied with the whole setup, while accepting the visitors' sincere compliments. Although they start off with the usual acknowledgements of the courtesy of being invited to our home, it is usually followed by the observation: 'Your residence conveys the essential character of a Moroccan home, in India.' For this compliment, I cannot, in all honesty, take the honours, or at least exclusively, because Karima has played the crucial role in making the space both true to its Moroccan character, and very welcoming for our visitors.

These compliments send my mind racing back to the family's, and more particularly my wife's, initial introduction to India in general, and to Delhi in particular. As with most newcomers, it had been the experience of massive crowds and proverbial traffic jams—a phenomenon we were totally unprepared for. Sitting in the car and driving to the residence from the airport or any place in the vast and densely populated city, she had anxiously enquired as to how far we would have to travel to reach the destination, and was told, 'Not very far, madam,' and yet her unbelieving eyes could only fathom the mass of humanity, along with waves of cars, with their additive pollution, all over the streets, aggravated usually by the lack of discipline among drivers. And, as one has assessed, this somewhat imposed conundrum makes the distance seem longer, demanding further patience.

And here I might generalise, somewhat accurately, that it is difficult to imagine with exactitude the times of arrival and departure to our destinations, due to the unpredictable nature of the road traffic. People tend to reach either before or after time, and find themselves victims of the adage "before time is no time and after time is no time; time is time".

In fact, all these elements and daily realities send me back automatically to the first statement of the then Dean of the Diplomatic Corps, the late Hans Castillanos, former Ambassador of the Dominican Republic. He had told me, at the airport, the day I arrived to Delhi as His Majesty's Envoy to India, in a subtle and pleasant way, the following statement, fraught with meaning, which I have never forgotten: 'When you come to India, dear Ambassador, if you are patient you will lose patience, but if you are impatient, you will learn, for sure, how to be patient.'

Even though I didn't take his advice for granted at that time—since I had visited India many times before and had a much better and more positive view about this vast country—I have started to find a good amount of truth in what he had implied, as time passes by. People here wouldn't equate the phenomenon of timeliness from a cultural point of view, as is the case elsewhere. In India, people would be inclined to take time over doing things properly, rather than being disposed to fulfil a clockwork calculation of time, especially when it comes to sharing moments with friends and family. Many would attribute this to the structure of Indian society. But for whatever reason, they do it, I personally believe that it makes their lives much easier, given the daily challenges they may face in mobility.

In fact, when it comes to traffic in the Indian capital, Karima would argue that the idea of having the luxury of travelling light—with just one's personal possessions to pack and unpack—

is a comfort that is usually denied to homemakers of Diplomatic families in big and distant challenging cities, like Delhi.

While reckoning on the time we have spent in India, allow me to digress a little from the above ramification, to capture and portray parts of the decor of our home. The setting of our reception spaces, where the Moroccan character has been consciously brought together, is imprinted with the most iconic craftsmanship of my country, namely our tradition of carpet weaving. The floor expanse is, thus, ornamented with this Moroccan weave traditionally and prevalently called "Zarbiya Rbatiya", meaning "Rabat Carpet", which is in a bright crimson, as well as some in royal blue—the two prevalent colours in their categories. The high knot density of the weave gives these floor coverings their rich feel and muted gloss. They are well coordinated with the arrangement of the furniture, which adheres to a typical Moroccan setting, converging around large centre tables, harking back to the custom of table settings for partaking meals as a community and familial ritual, in contrast to atypical Western-style drawing room decor.

Complementing the vivid spread underfoot is the collection of paintings that adorn the walls, both in the corridor and in the reception areas. Here, too, the Moroccan touch has been selectively displayed not for its artistic merit alone, but also for the depiction of traditional style in the painted portrayals. The central display, therefore, is a representation of the ancient Madrassa tradition of Islamic discourse, with the head of the gathering prominently placed and the other figures, in equally well-defined spaces, all harmonised together with the trappings of their calling. What is especially striking in this work, according to the impressionist school of painting, is the vivid colours of the turbans and other artefacts portrayed, so that the floor and the wall seem to be "knitted together" in a dialogue of Moroccan compliments that is *unmissable* by any visitor. It strikes me to see how intrinsically authentic it is, since just the sight of this painting sends me straight back to my tender age, when I used to attend the Quranic school along with my siblings and comrades of different ages.

Therefore, in the bright sunlit rooms of the residence in Delhi, it is but natural that the vibes visitors feel are that of the Moroccan tradition of making guests feel welcome and warmly comfortable under our roof. Delving deeper into our lifestyle, I would like to mention my wife's insightful manner and observations. These have been more grounded, as she has taken pains to project the hand of friendship, even while embodying perfectly our culture and origin, under our roof and that too, *au naturel*. In fact, she often describes these courtesies as being the *"amana"*, a deposit of trust conferred on our shoulders and which she gamely has transformed into a pleasurable fulfilment.

And it is not simply in the way of encompassing hospitality that my wife has put herself forward. Her committed interactions with welfare and charity organisations here have brought her in close contact with various strata of Indian women, and have drawn her into the commonalities existing in the two societies. Thus, she would often remark to visitors, 'I was struck by the many similarities between our two cultures and peoples, and the harmony that characterises our two ancient nations. I find that we share the same joy in offering hospitality and, more importantly, the value given to guests, elders and relatives in homes.' Then, in an outreach of utter frankness, she also reflects on the fact that 'the deference to traditions is becoming more difficult to preserve. Although young families usually lived with their parents in the traditional manner, however, the winds of change have started blowing, and young girls and boys, nowadays, prefer to be independent, as much as they can, except when there is no other choice, or due to lack of resources.'

WHAT IF... WHY NOT?

Another significant connection that Karima has found to be engaging our two cultures is the Indian *sari*, which has become a "symbolic link". The yardage of *sari* material has been admirably adopted by Moroccan fashionistas for their purpose. The heavily worked and sequined *sari* borders are used to "dress up" the lower end of the *takchita* or *caftan*, while the ornate *sari* end or *"pallu"* comes in handy for detailing the work of the upper portion of the garment. Then, with either a belt in golden or in silver tones, the attire is complete and decorous. But, while the *sari* has proved to be a charming bonding resource, it has not lightened our wardrobes because we still have to do the stitching and the weaving for the dresses we need to bring with us. These would end up being part of our personal collection of Moroccan costumes to wear, especially for occasions.

On the other hand, she would add that, while we, as a family relish the delight of an Indian spread of *biryani* and *kebab*, the Moroccan cuisine being a well-known brand worldwide, our food larder needs to be stocked with Moroccan indigenous ingredients that are hard to come by, in many overseas places, as well as on the subcontinent. There is also our special food, particularly dried ingredients that are a must. We use dried fruits like apricots, figs, and orange blossom water, almond sweets, and not to forget, large quantities of Moroccan mint-infused tea. We use olive oil, argan oil and, for good measure, I had also brought along couscous and sardines, not being sure of getting these items on arrival in Delhi.

When it comes to our daily routine, once the initial hurdles had been overcome, which had included a change of residence in early 2019 from the earlier one to one which was more in the nature of personal preferences, the family has realised the plus points of our new Indian home. The sprawling greenery of the surrounding compound immediately intensifies positivity. It comprises several manicured lawns, clusters of plumeria and mature allamanda plantings in the inner courtyards overlooking the reception areas, as well as the welcoming ground covered in beds of crocuses, hemmed around the entrance. Naturally, the home has begun to attract the avian variety of the city. Karima has always enjoyed gardens. 'I began to observe the things around the garden while seated in the glazed interiors, and found that our garden alone was attracting a good number and variety of birds at various times of the day and according to seasons.' This was her observation when we, the family members, shared some time together in the space.

Searching for other points of interest from the Indian chapter of our lives, *Madame* also likes to recount the learning episodes she faced on first setting up a house for the family. 'I was surprised at the working rules for the serving staff in the house. If, for instance, the person was a gardener, he would not be seen in the inner parts of the house, and just in case he was required to do so, he would make sure to remove his footwear and enter the home barefoot! Something I somehow admired. Then, if a person was to sweep the spaces, another was to clean the glass windows and doors, but imagine how I shocked the others by picking up the brush and tending to these chores personally. It was hilarious and culturally unacceptable and hardly proper for "the boss's wife". In fact, the people meant for the job felt almost insulted, as if they had failed in their duties, while it is simply a matter of habit. Cultures and the way each one does these things requires patience and tactful manners to make them accept all this'.

She would add, 'Somehow, there was no choice as things are to be done the way they should be, or rather the way we, Moroccans, are used to and taught to observe. The residence is a territory of Morocco, and it is the image of the country which is to be preserved. What really matters are the results, not the means.

WHAT IF... WHY NOT?

'And then there was the fathoming of dietary requirements of the guests we invited,' Madam likes to recount. As is often the case, her first venture at entertaining was a group of seven VIP guests in Delhi, most of whom were Indians. They were invited in honour of a Moroccan dignitary visiting Delhi, H. E. Mohamed Benaïssa, the former Minister of Foreign Affairs and Cooperation. The gathering included a few common friends, like the honourable Shashi Tharoor, who has become a close friend since then, Mr Swashpawan Singh, the Head of the Office of the then Vice President, H. E. Hamid Ansari, and the then Dean of the Diplomatic Corps. It was not at all a piece of cake as it should have been. Every small detail added to the difficulty of the task.

'It was a Tuesday, and one of the guests announced that besides being a vegetarian, on Tuesdays he did not partake of any onion or garlic-based dishes either. Another guest, unfortunately, was allergic to carrots, and another could not eat food prepared in butter! Adding to this confusion, one of them stated that he adopted a "no salt meal practice" on Tuesdays, resulting in me having to prepare six or seven dinners, instead of just one, for the evening. Last, but not least, was "a complete vegetarian", in that he did not partake of foods that were obtained from tubers growing below the soil, such as potatoes, yams and the like. In one single table, there was too much confusion. Thus, serving each one individually, while remembering their preferences, was no fun at all. It was done, and everybody was happy. The truth is that nobody knew the chaos in the minds of those behind the scenes. We learned, at least, that Tuesday was a day to be avoided for hosting at home, unless there was no other choice. All this was a learning process, which is in itself a way of being anything but simple! Patience again was the clue; then comes the clarity of mind.'

Yet, this was not the first or only instance of social challenges thrown at her. My first posting in Cameroon, which incidentally was the start of our homemaking as a diplomat couple, is an experience which *Madame* recalls vividly. It began with her not knowing a single word in English because she had done her education in Arabic and French, and her higher studies in the German language. As Cameroon is a bilingual country, using both English and French as official languages, she could foresee that despite being fluent in French, the lack of English would limit her interactions. Hence, she registered herself at the British Council in Yaoundé to learn the contemporary *lingua franca*. Besides her, several other young diplomats had brushed their language skills there. Thereafter, the self-learning process also kicked off, in large measure gaining momentum over the years.

'In Cameroon, we had a small Embassy of four diplomats. Also, the Moroccan Ambassador there, Mohamed Benomar, was very understanding of my situation and encouraged me in every possible way. In fact, he had often overlooked the protocol precedence of table arrangements at dinners at the residence by giving me the coveted honour of being seated next to him at the table. This allowed us to observe and learn how to receive and entertain guests'.

While hosting her first meal under our roof in Cameroon, *Madame* recalls smilingly how she had begun preparations for it, a week in advance, because 'Our table should reflect the generosity of the people of our country. Although we find it a bit excessive what we offer, in comparison to that of many others, we still somehow can't change, but cherish… so much is the pleasure.'

Hence, it would be a whole week of stress for her, learning new dishes at the young age of twenty-three. But she never gave up, though the experience was so new to her. We now laugh at the time it took to prepare for such an event, in comparison with the time it takes these days, when we receive guests with varying preferences and tastes. But still, the table would be no less loaded and colourful!

So, while looking back on her own journey, one can only doff one's cap and express admiration for the spouses of diplomats and to Karima, mainly, who can meet different challenges with creativity and aplomb.

By now, a seasoned handler of "social emergencies" of this sort that have been cropping up now and then, *Madame* likes to acknowledge the role of her better half, too, who is *yours sincerely*. 'For instance, there was the episode of a bomb blast in Karachi, an earthquake in Islamabad and, of course, Covid-19 and many other challenging moments in our lives. All these eventualities brought us closer together as a family, and since he loves doing something called "work", he is much more the "moral support" by and large, instead of the more hands-on addition to family matters. I also feel it is part of the family's conditioning, as he was not used to seeing his father or uncles in these roles, apart from the weekly shopping, which they handled. Thus, our "together time" is more for travelling, watching movies, or playing table tennis, billiards, swimming or shopping... But these times remain too short in a person's life. However, while travelling or on holidays, we are almost together the twenty-four hours of a day', she would sometimes share with her close friends, when exchanging observations about their families and daily matters.

On my own part, during the occasional musings that I indulge in, I have told myself the changing situations that we have had to cope with have permeated deep into our life as a family. For instance, our thinking during the mid-nineties is not quite what it is currently, as we have gone through our lives with expected and unexpected moments as a couple. Even our first meeting with each other was not a customary affair, as we are not related. We met at a hospital. It was at a time when her sister, Laila, had fallen sick and had to be admitted to the Military Hospital of Rabat for a long time.

Madame ruminates, saying, 'Laila had been together with a batch of army students, along with my would be husband, from the Foreign Service, at the Eighth International Conference on AIDS and HIV; the convention being held in Marrakesh, Morocco, in December 1993. The members had been involved in ensuring that the protocol duties during the conference were mainly for VIPs. I remember that the design of the logo for AIDS was most probably revealed in my country, as we all saw it first at the inauguration of the event, attended by more than four thousand participants. By the way, the logo, when it was used in Morocco, was an inverted symbol of the Arabic word (ال) "la" meaning "No" to AIDS. Unfortunately, most people use it nowadays in reverse and no longer as it used to be in 1993, symbolising collective efforts to fight against the disease, as well as extending support and compassion for those living with it.

'After they returned from the conference, the different participants remained in touch. When he learned about the illness of my elder sister, Laila, he paid a visit to her in the hospital, along with a small group of army students. But the next meeting was somewhat "heaven-sent" as he had come alone to visit and check on her again. While driving his car, a wheel got punctured on the way and had to be replaced. He walked into the hospital with dirty and soiled hands. It was natural that he washed them, but the running water was out of order for a while as the system was undergoing some maintenance. As he was shy, he washed them quickly; I could see they were not properly cleansed. I had given him some of our stored water and soap to wash his dirty hands more thoroughly. He had tried to be economical with the supply, and I had insisted that the shy young man should wash his hands thoroughly because we had enough water. Thereafter, my sister had left for France, but he would call me often to make enquiries about her and we had started talking.'

Yet, there were still some matters to be talked over between us. The habit of having to make adjustments in one's personal life to accommodate the family had been a prerequisite for this relationship to flourish, as my wife revealed to a journalist friend. Indeed, my family came from the south-east of the country, known as Tafilalet, where the local practices were distinctly different from hers, as ours were inclined towards a more conservative lifestyle. Thus, managing and making the necessary changes to suit the new circumstances has been the motto she has lived by, even today. This has been so in every country and every place we have gone to, making every new house, anywhere, become a home to be lived in for her family, as well as to provide a welcoming window for visitors to imbibe our culture and hospitality, in the true Moroccan tradition.

Of course, as mentioned earlier, the scale of duties as the wife of the Ambassador is on another level as it is not limited to receiving and welcoming people only, but also socialising, accompanying her spouse to state banquets and government receptions, and being involved in many activities in the host country. In fact, the spouse has a dual responsibility, and the representation can sometimes be equally important, if not more, in terms of impact. While we care mostly about the official side of the representation, the wives take care of all the other aspects, which may include, but are not limited to, social work, charity engagement, important events, and so on.

In this regard, it would be fair enough to add that she is not only on the managing committees of some of the important welfare and social associations in Delhi, but is also chairing or co-chairing a few of them. Incidentally, she has been for two terms, the President of the Spouses of the Heads of Mission (SHOM) in India, one being presently ongoing, while being three times co-Chairperson of the DCWA (Delhi Commonwealth Women's Association). She is also the Vice Chairperson of the Association of the Spouses of the African Heads of Mission (ASAHOM). All this would not have been possible without her personal commitment and dedication to whatever she undertakes, alongside her already heavy and highly demanding other duties, including the routine family ones.

I have always believed that the pressure on the spouses of diplomats is higher than that on the diplomats themselves. We do care most of the time, about work and official obligations only, but they care for our family and comfort. I shall always be indebted to my wife, Karima, and her exemplary dedication to the entire family and to the education of our two daughters. This makes me feel at times guilty of depriving all of them of together time and, above all, from what they love most back home, the larger family; the only reason behind this shortcoming being their "obligation" to follow me wherever I am posted, which I have always taken for granted, though it should not be so. For their unconditional support and tolerance, I will always be obliged to what I like to call my three ladies, Karima, Ghita, and Nada, along with my mother, adding the essence. I am blessed to have them all in my life; they are the essential and the precious part of it.

Narrating a small portion of the life of my spouse is not an objective in itself. It is basically meant to pay her tribute and highlight, at the same time, the important role that the spouses of diplomats can play in the career of their better halves. Their contributions should not be ignored by any means. Diplomacy remains a demanding and all-consuming job, in that it requires a minimum knowledge, besides acquiring diplomatic skills, which usually come with time and along with refining experiences.

With the passing of time at the helm of diplomatic affairs, we manage matters and face challenges more delicately and professionally. There are things I do and decisions I take that I could never have done earlier. This evolution has been equally apparent in Karima. That is why I firmly believe that the earlier the spouses of diplomats are involved in the activities, the easier life of a diplomat becomes. This is naturally an appeal to my younger colleagues not to ignore this part in their careers, as the returns on such an investment remain, at least for me, priceless.

Chapter 16

The Pride of Belonging

In the lives of people and countries, history matters, as I believe that it defines a certain identity and belonging. History also gives answers to numerous questions which help in understanding and differentiating people, not only as "distinct entities" but also in referring to them collectively as sharing a strong common identity and heritage. They all make the diversity of our world. Within this diversity, there are a few countries which have, through their rich history and culture, cultivated a strong identity by which they can live independently from other nations. In fact, the people of these countries are those who can live thoroughly by their own culture and traditions, be it food, dress, costumes, art, architecture, languages, and customs, if they were to decide one day to close their borders and live inwardly. It is a source of great pride to belong to the Kingdom of Morocco, one of these blessed countries. Moroccans are identified indeed by a multitude of things, which no one can miss.

When I notice people in their national dress, or in the dress of their region, it strikes me how the culture of the land or the wearer is reflected through the manner in which they have dressed. They are immediately recognised by their dress as a unique identity, distinguishing them from others. An Indian or a Moroccan, to name but these, would certainly resonate more with my observations about the traditional dress, as the mode of dressing in both countries is distinctive and culturally oriented.

Talking about this observation takes me back to February 2017, during the ceremony of presentation of my Letters of Credence to the former President of India, late Pranab Mukherjee, along with three more Ambassadors, from Tunisia, Yemen, and Zambia, respectively. All the people noticed that my spouse Karima and I were the centre of attraction owing to our traditional three-piece elaborate and hand-stitched attire. Ghita, my elder daughter, was also wearing a two-piece *caftan*. We could not have passed by unnoticed wherever we were.

On occasions like this, and in the presence of Heads of State, we are dressed in the highest official attire, exactly the way we do when we receive, in a very solemn ceremony, our Letters of Credence, directly from the hands of His Majesty the King. Despite the minute details to be observed and discomfort at times we may have, while wearing the dress, especially during warm weather, you are simply so overwhelmed by a feeling of pride and uniqueness, that one could give anything to preserve this tradition. The challenge remains, however, to keep all the pieces of the puzzle exactly as they should be worn, for a long time. Expressions of admiration over the attire I was wearing could be seen on the faces of people present in the audience, granted to me by the Honourable President on this occasion.

This inner excitement, mixed certainly with pride, but with a bit of reserve and apprehension at times, was conspicuous during all the ceremonies of presentation of my Letters of Credence to all the Heads of State of the four countries I am accredited to, besides India, in the region: Bhutan, Maldives, Nepal and Sri Lanka. In Nepal, I can never forget how people wanted to take a photo with Madam and me, dressed that way, while riding on a carriage pulled by horses, towards the Presidential Palace in Kathmandu, in a memorable and distinguished procession for the official ceremony. The same feeling of pride was experienced in all the other capitals during similar ceremonies, despite differences in the ceremonial processions, reflecting the history and customs of each nation distinctly.

As Moroccans, we also have a lighter attire that we wear on other official events we organise, like the reception we offer on the occasion of the celebration of the Enthronement Day, on the 30th of July, every year, the date of the accession of His Majesty King Mohammed VI to the throne of his glorious ancestors. It is also worn when we are invited to the official reception that Heads of State offer, like that on the occasion of the Republic Day celebrations in India. In such formal events, we usually wear a *Djellaba* and put on the red cylindrical cap known as *"Fez"*. In my country, people also wear this on Fridays, or on religious Eid days as well. Few put it on as a daily dress without raising particular curiosity from the others. In that sense, this dress is not exceptional as it remains part of our daily life. Yet, outside the country, it becomes a signature and a national identity, like a passport. The events I am going to share illustrate how important it is to have a distinctive identity.

In January 2018, or more precisely on the 26th, I was invited, along with my spouse, like all other Heads of Mission, Cabinet Members, High-Ranking Army Officers, and dignitaries in New Delhi, to the yearly reception organised at Rashtrapati Bhavan (the official residence of the President of the Republic) on the occasion of India's Republic Day celebrations. The event was being hosted by the then President of India, His Excellency Ram Nath Kovind. It was an opportunity to meet ministers and high officials, discuss and exchange current issues with my colleagues, representatives of different countries in India, where there is a large and active diplomatic community of more than one hundred and sixty missions, from different continents and parts of the world, besides a number of International Organisations.

After the official ceremony was over and at a certain time in the course of this interesting conversational exchange, the Honourable Indian Prime Minister, Shri Narendra Modi, who was dressed in an elegantly fashionable traditional Indian manner, was moving towards the guests. His bodyguards were covering all sides and the space ahead of him, forcing their way through the crowd to free more space for the dignitary, while he was busy returning the greetings of the crowd and exchanging pleasantries in a very relaxed and jovial manner. His movement and walk among the crowd with his bodyguards in tow attracted the attention of all people present at the event, many of whom were rushing to get as close to him as was allowed, for a photo opportunity. Several Ambassadors, including myself, and many Indian officials in the crowd, were waiting to greet him.

Everyone around suddenly became busy taking selfies with him from a distance. I can't deny that I was also waiting to have the best angle to seize the opportunity to get a good one. I recall that I was standing about two or three meters away with three other Ambassadors when I suddenly heard the Indian Prime Minister turn in my direction, saying, 'Ambassador, we can never ever miss you.' I thanked him, but exclaimed: 'I hope, it is in a positive way, Excellency!'

'Of course, we can't miss a Moroccan with his dress from afar, among all these people.'

'That is a kind thought of Your Excellency. I hope you like it, sir!' I humbly exclaimed.

'Of course, who doesn't? It is very elegant and unique,' he commented, smiling.

Overwhelmed, I didn't remember how I said to him, without really thinking, 'Does it mean Excellency that you wanted to have a photograph with me?'

'Why not? That sounds nice. Let's have it.' He replied, with a big smile on his face, to my great satisfaction.

Here, I can assure you that everything stood still for a while, and his nearest bodyguard asked me to join the Prime Minister for a photo. As you can imagine, in this kind of very official ceremony, we are usually advised to leave our mobile phones outside. Without giving this restriction a thought, at the least, I got hold of my mobile, in my pocket, and eagerly requested the nearest person in the crowd, an Indian lady, to take a photo of me with the star of that day, His Excellency Narendra Modi. While the photo was being taken, he enquired about the health of His Majesty and requested me to convey his heartfelt greetings to our King, Mohammed VI.

In that instance, I realised the importance of one's attire and the case of one's identity from among a crowd of people. I recall how his bodyguard had asked for a little more space all around us for the memorable photo. At that moment, the Prime Minister placed his right hand around my waist. Of course, in my excitement, I, too, reciprocated by placing my hand around his, as if he were a close friend of mine, when, suddenly, a firm and deep voice said: 'Sir, he can, but you can't.' Once the photo was shot, and sincere thanks were expressed to the Prime Minister for his kind gesture, I turned to the bodyguard and whispered to him jokingly, 'I will remove you from the photo, and you will have trouble with the *big boss*, thinking that you were not nearby him,' a promise that I kept, owing to professional editing and technology!

Indeed, his face—which was prominently in the middle between us—was simply erased from the original snap, as if he had never been there. Then, I printed a large copy of the picture, put it in an elegant frame and sent it, with a word of thanks and appreciation, to the Office of the Prime Minister. However, removing my hand, as I was ordered, didn't diminish or reduce, in the least, the beauty of the moment and of the photograph. I took what I thought to be the best shot among the crowd and a very fine photograph of that moment of identity between our two nations, through our representative national attire.

As he went ahead to greet other guests, my mind was filled with the thankfulness of how the cultural heritage of my country had singled me out of the crowd and given me this almost divine gift, being a holder of a universally known and recognised identity. It can't be anything other than a blessing from God.

It so happened, incidentally, that in the following year, too, on the same occasion at Rashtrapati Bhavan, New Delhi, the Honourable Prime Minister was, as usual, moving among the crowds of invitees, exchanging greetings with people. I have always admired his elegance and the way he is dressed. As I was absorbed in a conversation with my French counterpart, I didn't see the big movement the Prime Minister was creating around us, and, certainly, I was unprepared for what followed, as he was heading towards our direction.

I was wearing a grey-black striated *Djellaba*, made of wool, with different silk design work. As he approached me, he surprised me by saying, 'You look different this time, Ambassador.' I was astounded by his accurate observation and sharp memory. I replied spontaneously in a pleasant manner, 'Thank you, dear Excellency, I feel truly humbled. Don't tell me, sir, that you wanted another photograph with me again, this time!' He smiled and looked quite relaxed, yet with a hidden inquisitive smile. He was apparently amused at my quick reaction and at the inverted roles I tried to play and the joke I cracked, almost without thinking, making my wish look like his own.

In fact, while posing for the photograph, he remarked, addressing the nearby crowd, to the astonishment of all those who heard him: 'He always makes me laugh!!'

Everybody could see how thrilled I was by this observation, for which I thanked him dearly. I had jumped at this second opportunity coming my way and had clicked yet another landmark occasion of identity, as a Moroccan in my national makeover.

The national identity factor, through one's cultural makeover, came to the forefront when I accompanied my Secretary of State to the audience that the Prime Minister had granted to both of us, on the occasion of the Third Gujarat Summit, in early March 2019. Morocco, which was a Country Partner of the Summit, was represented by a big delegation with two Ministers, one for commerce and industry and the other for higher education. The Ministerial Delegate from Morocco to the summit, Madame Rokia Edderham, was easily noticed and identified as she was wearing the Moroccan dress from her region. As she was a resident of the Moroccan Sahara region, she was dressed in a *M'Lehafa*, which is a long, single-piece dress worn by ladies of that region, making them look superbly feminine and decent. Her attire not only exuded the culture of my land but went a step further because it reflected the diversity of Morocco through the different regions of the country.

Once again, there was an exchange with the Honourable Prime Minister when he pointed out: 'Your Minister, Ambassador, is more Moroccan than you are today.' Indeed, I was wearing a Western suit for the occasion. Taking this opportunity to clarify my stand, I had ventured to explain: 'Sir, I could never dream of competing with a lady, and it is never my intention to steal the honour justly due to my Minister!'

'He always finds the right words,' he exclaimed with a smile, without looking in my direction or saying any further remark.

The matter had soon passed, but it left me proud of my Minister and the preservation of our cultural identity. During that audience, I could see he liked the way I had freed myself from his challenging remark. During the few seconds that the setup and the photo shoot took, he once again asked us to convey his warmest and fraternal greetings to His Majesty. After the meeting, and as you can imagine, I had to explain to my Minister, later, the meaning behind his initial remark. She was quite happy with the small anecdotes I had shared with the Prime Minister.

But the biggest surprise awaited me six days later when, once again, on the Republic Day reception, in the lawns of Rashtrapati Bhavan, I was exchanging pleasantries with other Ambassador colleagues when the Indian Prime Minister stopped to greet different dignitaries and foreign Envoys. This time, it was more organised in the sense that there was a protocol rope put along his passage. After having given my wife my phone, I asked her to be prepared for the photo, as this time, I knew he wouldn't stop for a long time. So, I went and stood in the place where I knew he would pass by. Two of my colleagues were insisting on sticking to me because they knew the Prime Minister might stop nearby, like he had done in the previous two years, for a photo souvenir with me.

So, honestly, when the Prime Minister stopped and greeted me warmly, there wasn't much space to take a relaxed photo like before. While he was greeting me, I didn't hesitate to tell him, 'Dear Sir, with all my deepest respect, I wonder if I could have the honour to take another photo with you as I have become quite used to collecting pictures with Your Excellency.' I remember his answer was, 'It is always with pleasure, Ambassador. Besides, you have a different attire every time. You have a wonderful culture and very elegant dresses.'

'So do Indians—and Your Excellency in particular,' did I say. And thus, another photograph was taken with him, for the third consecutive year.

Only the different attire we both were wearing and those brief but exceptional moments immortalised through the photographs taken could reveal that they were captured at different moments on the same occasion, each being taken exactly one year after the other. The scary side is that we don't seem to be conscious of how time flies. Though it may appear slow, it is *not*.

On every occasion with the Prime Minister on Republic Day, I became more conscious of the importance of culture in our lives and in making traditions last. At that moment, I was temporarily transported into the realm of my own thoughts. I became aware of how two old nations, like India and Morocco, can be identified and distinguished from any other individual in the entire world simply by their mode of dressing, the complexity of their manufacture, the hand-weaving and the finish.

Moreover, some might ask: 'Anybody wearing a *Djellaba* is not necessarily a Moroccan'. To them, I would venture to retort that the Moroccan *Djellaba*, worn by both men and women, is made special by intricate embroidery. Hence, it has been part of us for ages and has continuously stood the test of time with the same strength.

WHAT IF... WHY NOT?

It is not without a special feeling of pride for me that my predecessors, such as those Moroccan Ambassadors who were appointed to the courts of Europe, as far back as the end of the sixteenth century, were dressed in the Moroccan attire, similar to the one we wear today, albeit with slight differences. We put on this attire currently, on most official occasions, as in the opening session of the Parliament, or during the ceremony of receiving Letters of Credence from His Majesty the King.

I would take the example of the Ambassador Abdel Ouahed Ben Massoud Ben Mohammad Anoun, who was the Principal Secretary to the Moroccan ruler, Sultan Ahmed Al-Mansour. Ambassador Anoun was recognised as an eminent figure with outstanding diplomatic skills, to the extent that his portrait, worked in the oil-on-wood technique, is still displayed at the Shakespeare Institute, located in Shakespeare's Stratford-upon-Avon. It forms a key addition to the collection of the University of Birmingham, and widens, at the same time, the scope of Shakespeare studies, among others.

The portrait itself, in its strikingly life-like technique, was painted in the subject's 42nd year, as is indicated by the number "42" clearly visible in the work. It depicts the emissary in full diplomatic attire, complete with *Djellaba, Selham,* and a ceremonial sword, and is ranked as the only Tudor era portrait of a Muslim. It came into the open market in the fifties and was spotted by the Institute's Director. Even today, this portrait has not lost its importance for this illustrative work, in formal Moroccan regalia. It also formed a key part of the exhibition "The Tudors: Art and Majesty in Renaissance England", which was on view at the Metropolitan Museum of Art, the Cleveland Museum of Art, and San Francisco's Legion of Honor, USA, proving once again how personal makeover can live on, through the right choice of one's national attire.

According to official records, Sultan Al-Mansour had appointed Ambassador Anoun to the Court of Queen Elizabeth I of England in 1600, in her 42nd year of reign. The envoy had led an Embassy composed of 16 people, including an interpreter, and a few English prisoners who were being returned to the Crown of Britain as a gesture of goodwill. Mr Anoun's primary mission was to reinforce trade relations and diplomatic links between Morocco and Britain, at that time, a time when most of the countries we know of today didn't yet exist, or at least, not in their current forms and borders. The Ambassador had arrived at the Elizabethan court and had stayed for half a year, where his task was also to forge a full-scale military alliance with Her Majesty's kingdom.

On a lighter note, while this Ambassador was sent to deepen trade and diplomatic ties, it is generally believed that he had influenced Shakespeare in his depiction of "Othello", who, too, is described as being of Moorish origin, in the play. But the linkage goes no further. I wanted to underline that he was dressed in a *Djellaba* under the *Selham*, a long, loose overgarment, generally of wool, which Moroccans usually wear, over a *Djellaba*, for different reasons, like official occasions, or in severe winters. We still dress in the same manner at the highest official occasions. Therefore, I am so happy that our culture has survived, owing to the Moroccans being deeply wedded to their ancient traditions, heritage, and handicrafts.

In the different forms of attire that I have the privilege to wear as Head of Mission on occasions, I have come to realise that any of my traditional attires at their different levels of formal codes and complexity is the best example to represent my country. The wearer who is immediately recognised as being a Moroccan need not utter a single word to reveal his identity.

Furthermore, the uniqueness of Moroccans is not limited to the traditional wear for both males and females, used on a daily basis, or on special occasions, but it goes far beyond that. It also encompasses the singular and inimitable architecture, which has become a fashion and a sought-after design worldwide, since people want a Moroccan adorned character, with precise gypsum work in the interiors of their private homes.

The cuisine, vouched to be among the top in the world, as rated number one by the Michelin-starred British Chef Gordon Ramsay, among others, is yet another typical aspect of the Moroccan culture. Indeed, whenever *"tagine"* is mentioned—among many other linkages—it sends you straight to the well-established and recognised Moroccan art of culinary tradition and its refined know-how, which hasn't undergone many changes for centuries.

On the handicraft side, the acquired expertise has advanced remarkably in many areas. If I take only the example of the art of leatherworking, it existed already in the 11th century, and has now developed to the extent that the refined leather goods in the world are called *"la maroquinerie"*—a term derived from *'Maroc'* in French.

Music is another aspect where Morocco has a strong footprint and these kinds of music don't exist elsewhere. I particularly mention Andalusian music, Ahwach, El Malhoun, and Gnawa. I can go on and on, displaying the different and unique facets of this rich culture.

As part of my own nature, I have no desire to speak extensively on this subject. Nonetheless, I find myself somehow compelled to say a few lines about Morocco's contribution to the human civilisation in terms of learning and knowledge, in its broad sense. In this regard, it is worth reminding that the oldest existing, continually operating, University is Al-Qaraouiyine, which was built in 859 CE, in Fes. The City of Fes is considered to be the spiritual and cultural capital of Morocco, and is one of its four Imperial Cities. It was also the political capital before the advent of the French protectorate in 1912.

The credit for building this world-renowned institution goes to a woman of knowledge and courage, "Assayida" Fatima Al Fihriya. The University remains unique by having outstanding architecture, symbolising refined artistic craftsmanship, comprising geometric patterns, in tiles, in plaster work and in wood carving. Even the large perforated brass chandeliers were and still are made in Morocco and have become a signature item. Academically speaking, it has had since then, and still has, one of the richest libraries from the ancient Muslim world, comprising rare books and manuscripts. Al-Quaraouiyine University has offered to its students, across many centuries, different and diverse disciplines. The courses have included Islamic studies, mathematics, grammar, astrology, medicine, and many more. This University had the honour to deliver the first-ever degree (*ijaza*) in the world in medicine and veterinary disciplines, as far back as the year 1207 CE.

These different aspects of the Moroccan identity that enrich the cultural and historical heritage of an entire nation are something very deep and defined in a wordless, but unmistakable way. I am, as all Moroccans surely are, deeply proud to uphold this unique distinctiveness and to consider it, by all means, a gift from God.

Chapter 17

A Uniquely Built Friendship

My posting to India was a great honour for my whole family, but more particularly for me, as I have mentioned many times earlier, yet I can't avoid repeating it. I knew how important it was to be given the opportunity—treasured at its real value—to serve as the Ambassador of His Majesty the King of Morocco to the great country of Gandhi, whose teachings had transcended the borders of his own land. Nonetheless, I can hardly hide how it struck me at the outset as a heavy and even "extensive" responsibility. My mandate cover also Bhutan, Nepal, the Maldives, and Sri Lanka. Hence, before joining New Delhi and assuming my new duty, I had decided to do some homework in preparation for the responsibility ahead, while making the final arrangements for travel with my family.

When I was appointed, I realised that there were members of the Government of His Majesty with whom I was acquainted and had worked more closely than other Ministers. I also believed they were more familiar with the country, its economic potential and the possibilities it would offer in terms of economic cooperation, investment, and bilateral relations, which should include, but not be limited to, connecting with governments and institutional officials, important private groups, their CEOs, Indian prominent businessmen, and industrialists. Therefore, my preparatory actions, prior to landing on Indian soil, were to call on these Ministers, prominently with economic and technical portfolios, to discuss with them the perspectives of cooperation with India, and more importantly, to get an idea of what they would expect from me during my tenure.

Consequently, keeping in mind the importance of India economically and industrially, I made it a point to meet the then Minister of Industry, Commerce, and Digital Economy in the previous Government, Mr Moulay Hafid Elalamy. During the course of our conversation, I broached the query: 'Mr Minister, as you perfectly know, India is a vast country—and in fact it contains many *countries* called *states* within the same one, and all are under the same flag. What do you expect from me as an Ambassador, and especially, what could be of interest to the sectors under your portfolio?'

After expressing his appreciation of the initiative to get his views and perspectives, his ready answer, I must say, took me a little by surprise. While underlining the importance of India and its positive economic prospects in terms of growth and investment, and how central the country was for Morocco, as a partner, he said that we need to have quality Indian companies capable of bringing added value to our economy. He then unexpectedly said: 'We have been trying to invite Mr Ratan Tata to pay a visit to Morocco for a long time, but it hasn't materialised so far. It may be because we didn't put the necessary effort in this regard.' He further added that he was confident of my capacity to make this visit happen.

Probing a little further along these lines, I recall that I had inquired whether I was to introduce Mr Tata to the possibility of a potential investment in Morocco, or was I simply to extend an invitation to him to visit my country as a visitor. My Minister made things very clear and underlined that he did not expect me to broach any discussion on investments there, but simply to persuade Mr Tata to come to Morocco first as a visitor to see the country and the socio-economic development it was able to reach in the last two decades. He added in a teasing, ironic manner, 'If you manage to bring him, there would be no need to keep our Embassy there, in India, open.' Of course, I knew he didn't mean what he said—not in the least—but it was rather his manner of putting a bit more pressure on me while assigning me with this mission.

Naturally, this request, albeit a tentative possibility, seemed to be quite a challenge for me. I therefore gave a befitting and positive response to his request. I promised the Minister to do all I could to materialise this invitation as soon as possible. Outwardly, my remark pulsated with strong confidence, but inwardly, I thought to myself that the challenge of getting a person like Ratan Tata to Morocco was no easy task. Indeed, within myself, I believed that there was no need to rush things and that I should let this project take as much time as needed. Knowing myself to be a naturally persistent person, I decided that my approach to the task ahead would be to create the conditions for Mr Tata to come to Morocco, not by my dogged persuasion, but by his own conviction. In other words, his visit to my country should be primarily worthwhile and, even more importantly, a rewarding experience for him.

Thus, after settling down to my duties at my office in New Delhi, and prior to my presenting my credentials to the Honourable President of India, I made clear my intentions to my colleagues and requested my assistant to remind me about introducing a request to the office of Mr Ratan Tata that I wished to pay a courtesy call to him. I would also leave the acceptance of my request to Mr Tata as well as the timing of the call. So, one of my first assigned tasks in India had been set afloat with a "risky" endeavour, and I waited for the feedback on my request. Right during the week following the presentation of my Letters of Credence to the late President Pranab Mukherjee, a formal request was introduced to Mr Tata's office.

As I could have expected, all that I was given as feedback to my queries was that Mr Tata was travelling at that point in time... the agenda still didn't permit, and yet, they were still looking into the matter, and so on. I never lost patience, though the stretch of time from the moment of introducing the request, in February 2017, lengthened until, at last, after a few long weeks, I received a short note informing me that Mr Tata would be free to meet me at the end of May, or the beginning of June. Also, the time allotted for our meeting was severely limited to a courtesy call. We were told, 'Mr Tata would be pleased to meet the Ambassador of Morocco for 10 to 15 minutes.' Of course, I did not look the proverbial gift horse in the mouth, being concerned not with the duration but rather the materialisation of the meeting. Also, I believed that 10 to 15 minutes was good enough to convey what I had to say. Grasping the offer, and without having the slightest hesitation, I immediately accepted the narrow slot allocated for our meeting.

At minus one to "D-day", I flew to Mumbai with my colleague, Mr Hasan, who was the Deputy Head of Mission. He was given the important responsibility of keeping a hawk's eye on his watch and giving me an appropriate—but—discreet signal at the completion of ten minutes of my meeting so that I could wind up the conversation within the stipulated time limit, not exceeding the 15 minutes initially communicated. Of course, I, too, had done my "homework" before the scheduled meeting. Since my task had been cut out for me, I decided to find out what could possibly be the center or even centres of interest for my respected interlocutor, first, and then how to raise his interest, especially with regards to my country.

As you can imagine, I made it a point to reach the Tata Sons' building adequately before the time given to us. After being ushered to the waiting room and prior to our meeting, I spent my time thumbing through the pages of a magazine related to the wide range of Tata group activities in India and abroad. Suddenly, there was an atmosphere of stillness and a bizarre silence that fell all over the room and no more murmurs were heard. This distracted my mind from flipping through the pages of the magazine, pushing me to look up. To my great surprise, Mr Ratan Tata himself was standing there, right in front of me, and greeted me saying, 'It is a pleasure to meet you at last, Mr Ambassador.'

My feelings at that moment were not—in the least—those of a schoolboy excited at coming face to face with his favourite football star. On the contrary, it was a very emotional sentiment to be with one of those who count in our world. Apart from the tremendous contribution of his group to modern India, he, as a single human being, embodies overflowing humanity with endless philanthropic actions. To see him standing there, in front of me, in a very simple manner, with his legendary modesty, made me realise—what is important is not the container which carries something, but the content or the weight that is contained within the container. It was an indescribable moment, fraught with mixed feelings of pride and, of course, some apprehension, as this was the moment I had been waiting for. As you could expect, during the previous weeks, after the meeting had been fixed, my concern had been, naturally, the fear of wasting this opportunity that had come up, at last. And here it was, up to me to make the best use of the encounter, since it may never come up again.

A UNIQUELY BUILT FRIENDSHIP

Mr Tata immediately put me at ease and invited us into a cosy meeting room. There were two other people who accompanied us, Mrs Sanyogita Atrey, a businesswoman who had a housing project with the Tata group in the Maldives, and her assistant. She had promised to push also from her side to make the meeting happen. In fact, I later discovered that she would rather have been using me to meet Mr Tata as she had not been able to reach him by herself. But her presence didn't affect our meeting in the least.

I remember taking a very special gift to offer him. It was a traditional Moroccan musical instrument, the Rabab, a handcrafted piece, delicately put in a specially made box with elegant red velour inside. The Rabab has different forms, and its variations are found in many cultures. But in Morocco, it is used mostly, if not only, in Andalusian music. It is an instrument which was prevalent only in ancient civilisations and old nations. I could not think of a better connection between Morocco and India than the cultural heritage, embodied in this distinguished and symbolic artefact. The fingerboard of the instrument was ornamented with an intricate carving on brass, in true Moroccan artistry.

While offering it to him, I emphasised that, because he was a person who was not only sensitive to culture but contributed to its promotion, my hope was that he would find in this instrument a symbol of the valuable connection between our two nations. The instrument, I added, had been around in Morocco for a long time and had stood the test of time by keeping its initial form. It has been used in Andalusian music for many centuries. India also has similar instruments, but different in form and sound from the Moroccan one. I urged him to accept the instrument from a, hopefully, would-be friend. He liked the gift, and through the gift, he admired the finesse of Moroccan craftsmanship and the elegance of its culture. In fact, to my great satisfaction, the instrument sparked his curiosity to know more about the history of Morocco, and that left the doors wide open for our conversation on my country.

Meanwhile, the stipulated timing of 10 to 15 minutes for our meeting was of no more importance, though it was largely exceeded. And my deputy no longer needed to signal me after the first 15 minutes to wrap up the meeting. After the cultural interlude ended, serious matters started and I veered, when I felt it was timely, and in fact at his request, to the general economic information about Morocco and its implemented structural reforms, without placing too much focus on any particular sector. It was not and should not be the primary objective of this first meeting, I thought. I told him that as an Ambassador serving in India, I would have failed in my duties if I could not persuade him to look at Morocco, first, as an interesting tourist destination. I added that it would mean a lot if a person of his standing could undertake a trip to Morocco and allow us to welcome him as a special guest.

The meeting had stretched to 58 minutes to our mutual surprise, when I decided to wind up, not wanting to be a heavy guest. As the conversation went on and on, I felt his interest to know more about Morocco was growing, to my great contentment. As I excused myself, he spontaneously replied, 'it is still early.' I could guess that he hadn't realised how much time we had spent together. When I told him that we would very soon exceed an hour conversing, he said to my surprise and great satisfaction, 'I will let you go now, Ambassador, if you promise me that the next time you come to Mumbai, you will be my guest for lunch, or dinner.' Of course, I couldn't have wished for a better offer.

My second meeting was, as agreed earlier, around a copious meal he offered graciously to me when I visited Mumbai, a few weeks following our first meeting. I made sure he would be present at that time in the city, as my visit's main objective was to meet him. This two-hour-long lunch, marked by rich exchange and friendliness, took place at the chambers of the Taj Palace, my favourite hotel in the economic capital of India.

As you can imagine, this second meeting suddenly became, at least for me, more important and central than the first one because I was aware it would determine the future of our personal relations, which certainly would impact, either way, his perception of Morocco. In other words, he was discovering and looking at Morocco through me. The difficulty of the second meeting was whether the chemistry we both felt at the first meeting would be confirmed, especially with a person of this stature, whom no one should take for granted—busy all the time, with lots of experience, someone who would not be easy to convince, I thought.

My main purpose was, I believed, to remain authentic and natural. This would help me to, not only meet his expectations, but also, and more importantly, to personally live up to my aspirations, which at that time was to become friendly with this legend without imposing myself on him. I simply would not allow this to happen. That would in itself have been a success. In the course of the meeting, I was quite happy and surprised that he had extensively gone through, not only the documents I had left for him at the first meeting, but also those I had sent, later on, at his request.

Equally important, it was during lunch that the idea of visiting Morocco started to make its own way, in a smooth manner. Deep down, I was excited at the thought of the possibility of realising this important project. It became suddenly reassuring to see phrases like, 'If I go, what would I see? or 'How do you manage these things?' appearing in the middle of our friendly conversation and in a very relaxed atmosphere. I believe that the lunch ended on a highly positive note. On a personal level, I felt satisfied with the outcome as the time spent together allowed me to get to know Mr Tata more closely. It also allowed me to offer him a broader view of my country and to start discussion on his possible visit to Morocco in the near future. This reflection started to come up now and then smoothly in our exchanges.

As you can imagine, I made it a duty to keep my Minister in Morocco informed, step by step, about our meetings and especially on the progress made so far. Subsequently, after our third meeting, around dinner, I thought it right to ask the Minister to extend a formal invitation to Mr Tata to pay a private visit to Morocco. I received the requested letter in less than two days. I do admit that the Minister's prompt interaction, with regards to my demand, encouraged me to go further and gave me, naturally, more reassurance and confidence in the next steps that I needed to take. It also allowed Mr Tata to appreciate the development of our relations and to integrate his visit, eventually, into his future agenda. Therefore, after receiving the formal invitation, our two offices began exchanging possible and convenient dates for both parties to materialise this visit.

I recall how surprised Mr Tata was when I was accommodating all his *desires* and, whatever dates he proposed, my Minister and I would accept them positively. At a later date, Mr Tata would retrospect and tell me: 'I didn't find any more reasons not to undertake this visit. With every excuse to postpone it, you never demurred and would continue with quiet determination,' he commented kindly, while we were together in Morocco.

So, with regard to his visit, his office informed us that he could not afford more than two days and one night in Morocco as his agenda was quite hectic at the end of the year, 2017. After discussing this proposal extensively with my Minister, we concluded that I would gently inform Mr Tata that we preferred to postpone the visit in that case. My argument was that we would feel frustrated to see him come all that way for just a single night! I added, 'With such a big time difference, you would only feel exhausted and very disappointed, as everything in your visit would be done in a rush and would be pointless and even counterproductive.'

Since the first impression of a place is what remains engraved in our minds, I wanted to make sure that the trip would be surrounded by all the ingredients of success, instead of disappointments. He was kind enough to understand my worries and a new set of three days was proposed for January, 2018. My Minister insisted that I be part of the trip, and Mr Tata generously offered to take me along with him in his private jet. I gently declined, arguing that I would prefer to welcome him in Morocco, instead. I also wanted to make sure that all necessary arrangements were made to ensure a successful visit.

Incidentally, when his flight landed, it was planned that the landing would be in the special area dedicated to receiving business and private jets. Unfortunately, the private travellers' lounge and their jets' parking area were under renovation and the lights were not sufficiently bright as is the case in most airports. So, it was a little disappointing to think that Mr Tata, who was arriving at night, would first open his eyes on Moroccan soil in a gloomy area. On landing, therefore, a Senior Director and I went to welcome him and his assistant. They both were seated in a small room meant usually for the police and custom duties personnel only. The setting of the space was not of a standard befitting a guest of his stature, as it even had a luggage scanning machine stacked in a corner of the room! Even the Lady Protocol Officer in charge was at her wits end trying to find justifications and explain the circumstances to our distinguished guest. However, even if gestures of hospitality had been extended to him in this cramped place, our embarrassment was anything but inconspicuous. I thought the visit had started on the wrong foot.

On my part, I was watching Mr Tata and I could see in his eyes a kind of apprehension, a silent question: 'Where have I set foot? Was it really worthwhile to waste three precious days of my life in this lost place at the extreme north of Africa?' Later on, as we became closer friends he had confessed to having such thoughts. He even went on to say, 'When I decided to come it was because there was no other excuse left for me that could stand against travelling to your country. So just to please you, I had relented, but, at that particular moment at the airport', he confessed, 'I felt that I had taken a wrong decision by giving in to your persistence.'

Outside the VIP Police or Customs Room, on completion of the formalities, there were two large, luxurious cars, one for him and the other was for his assistant, a very nice and charming gentleman, Mr Vitin Karkhera, and a senior Director, Mrs Ayda Fathi, who was given the task of being the official Liaison Officer. En route, while heading towards the city of Casablanca and getting back to "civilisation", I could deduce that his worries started to gradually fade away, little by little, until we reached the Four Seasons Hotel, located by the seaside, near the heart of Casablanca. The structure of the hotel amused Mr Tata a lot, as it had four storeys below the ground level and the lobby was on the fifth floor, at eye level with the sea beyond. It was a unique configuration.

The programme of his three days' stay included initially visits to Casablanca, Tangiers, and Rabat. After our first dinner, we moved for coffee outside the lobby space into the outdoors and sat close by the chimney, on the veranda. The place was arranged with sofas all around the blazing fire, as the night was a bit chilly. While we were enjoying our drinks, a person walked up and enquired:

A UNIQUELY BUILT FRIENDSHIP

'Mr Ratan Tata in Morocco? What a lovely surprise. I can't believe my eyes. What brings you here, sir?' The person was an Indian residing in the United Kingdom who said that he had been coming to Morocco whenever he felt homesick. After taking a photo souvenir with him, he inquired: 'When are you going to Marrakech?'

'No, I am not going there' was Mr Tata's reply, hardly audible. Incidentally, another Indian with his wife joined us, and after requesting for a photo opportunity with this iconic and revered person, he also enquired: 'I hope, sir, you are visiting Marrakech?' Mr Tata answered him innocently, 'I won't be able to make it, as my programme is set and my time is unfortunately limited.' I could see in his face the unspoken words expressing a growing desire to visit this city that everybody strongly recommended.

Deep in my mind at that instant, I also wanted to have him see this city, which is classed as the *number one* destination in the whole of Africa! I didn't tell him anything on the spot, but I asked later on, that night, that Mrs Fathi initiate a "Plan B" to visit Marrakech as I had a feeling that he was too shy and hesitant to disturb the programme. During the dinner which Mr Alami offered in his honour, I shared with him the unspoken wish of Mr Tata to visit Marrakech. He instructed the lady to adjust the programme accordingly. The next morning, Marrakech was on and the visit to Rabat was no longer on the agenda, much to his satisfaction and surprise.

Without getting into the details of this visit, I can proudly say that it went very well. What Mr Tata said while flying together from Tangiers to Marrakech was very comforting: 'To be honest, I didn't expect Morocco to have reached such development in many fields.' He emphasised on the quality of the infrastructure, mainly. The episode at the airport was soon forgotten. At the end, Mr Tata understood and confessed that three days were too short to savour what this country had to offer in terms of opportunities as well as its rich, multifaceted culture and tourist attractions.

Unexpectedly, Mr Tata fell in love with Tangiers, most precisely the Mirage Hotel, while most people prefer the imperial city of Marrakech for its charms, handicrafts, cultural heritage and, above all, its historic character. I'm guessing it was the lovely sight of the sea from where one can see Southern Europe without any artificial equipment that cast its spell on him. It was a very clear and sunny day, and the place where we had lunch could not be anything but mesmerising as one could see the Mediterranean Sea merging with the waters of the Atlantic Ocean, with their nuanced colours of blue distinguishable to the naked eye. Even for me, who has seen it many times, it was breathtaking. I ruminated on the course of the Mediterranean Sea which has witnessed the rise and fall of so many civilisations, and then the Atlantic Ocean that took travellers and sailors far beyond, into the *unknown*.

Our stay in Marrakech was booked at La Mamounia Palace, the legendary heritage hotel filled with old world charm and expansive, luxuriously manicured gardens facing the Atlas Mountains. It is also universally known for its Churchill Suite on the third floor, a suite that bears the name of the former Prime Minister of Great Britain, as that is where he used to stay, mostly, during the six times he visited Marrakech, for a retreat to paint one of his most famous paintings "Tower of the Koutoubia Mosque". It was created during a visit with President Roosevelt after the Casablanca Conference in 1943. He described Hotel La Mamounia as "the most lovely spot in the world". It seemed he even painted from the balcony of his suite at the hotel.

However, spending the night there and almost two days, Mr Tata did not seem interested by the place because his mind was set on Tangiers, and this seemed to hinder his enjoyment of other places. One of the funny things he reported to me the next morning of our stay in La Mamounia was his morning shower, the cold and hot water taps being antique and not easy to balance. So, he would report, 'It is freezing at one time', and he would shiver while saying it, explaining amusingly. 'Again, without giving prior notice or time to adjust,' he would say, 'it is burning', making grimaces to express what I would describe as a perplexed astonishment. Of course, the trip was full of "visits" and "discoveries", particularly for him and also, to some extent, for me. I would summarise this visit again by using the words he used himself to describe it, 'It is an eye-opening visit'.

One unforgettable highlight for me and also the passengers on board, who enjoyed tremendously, were the funny stories and discussions we enjoyed during the flights on his Gulfstream from Casablanca to Tangiers, which we reached in no time. Then, I would never forget when we flew from Tangiers to Marrakech, facing the Atlas Mountains, dressed in a dazzling white gown with brownish, abstract geometric figures, on that mid-January day, in a breathtaking scenery, which I was admiring from the impressive cockpit of the G-650. We all could see from the sky how the country is so diverse and beautiful. 'It is beyond expression,' exclaimed one of the pilots.

The episode of his arrival in the middle of the night and the interrogations it raised became history and a funny story that we would recall and laugh over from time to time. We even started talking about when the next visit would take place. For me, these were unmistakable indications that his visit was a success and enjoyable too. My Minister and Mr Tata got along with each other very quickly, became friends and understood each other perfectly in an unexpected convergence of views and mutual understanding. They agreed that there would be "an after" to this visit for sure, either in Morocco, India, or elsewhere. For me it was a relief, and a real feeling of satisfaction after an accomplished risky mission I was entrusted with, one year back by my Minister.

The following day, after the visit was over and Mr Tata had left, I called the Minister to express thanks and appreciation for all the efforts and hospitality he had extended to all of us to make this first-ever visit of Mr Tata successful, smooth, and enjoyable. Then I added in a deeper, more sober voice, 'Mr Minister, I have a piece of unpleasant news to share with you this morning!' He seemed very disturbed and said, 'I hope all is fine on the family and health sides. What is it?' I told him that I had learnt from reliable sources that Morocco would break off its relations with India. He immediately retorted, 'How could it be possible? Everything seemed alright, and relations are developing steadily. Did anything serious happen politically between the two countries to justify this? I am not aware of such a thing.' Then I couldn't keep the suspense any longer and replied, 'Sir, a year back, one of the important Ministers, with a heavy portfolio, told me if I managed to bring Mr Tata to Morocco, we wouldn't need a diplomatic presence in India any more. Now that this visit has happened, there is no reason to keep it open.'

I could hear him laughing his lungs out. 'You fooled me. What a fright you gave me. Brilliantly put, I remember that the Minister was none other than me!' he said, still laughing. 'On the contrary, now we need you more than ever after such positive and encouraging developments. You have become a friend of Mr Tata; you can't leave him so soon,' adding, 'to tell you the truth, I was sure you would end up making it happen one day, knowing your perseverance. But honestly, I didn't expect it would materialise so quickly. Bravo and thank you,' he concluded. I couldn't admit more to him that without his personal, continuous, and full support, this visit would have probably never taken place.

But after this memorable visit, both Mr Tata and I felt that formality was no longer necessary between us. Thus, when I invited him on the occasion of the celebrations of the Enthronement Day of His Majesty, King Mohammed VI, in Delhi, on 30th July 2018, I was so thrilled to receive the confirmation of his presence on the very next day, an honour which I was told he had never done before. I was even more grateful to his friendship as he was keen to renew this gesture on the same occasion the following year. Even before leaving for Mumbai, when the manager of the Imperial Hotel, Delhi, where we celebrated the occasion, expressed the hope of having the honour of welcoming him the following year, 2020, he replied: 'I will come, if the Ambassador invites me.' Unfortunately, Covid-19 broke out meanwhile, and everything changed for everyone. However, when we decided to celebrate the event in a virtual setting, he didn't hesitate, at my request, to register a video message to be posted on the occasion among other messages from a few other dignitaries from the political, economic, diplomatic, and academic spheres.

On a personal note, I would always wonder what could move a person of the stature of Mr Tata to mobilise his private jet and dedicate his precious time to come along from Mumbai just to attend our celebrations, except a genuine friendship and a tremendous mutual respect for each other. His friendship, the warmth and affection he has always shown to me and to my family, are truly priceless and something that I will always cherish. Indeed, I will be indebted to him for his kindness and soul-generosity, hard to find elsewhere. Life has also taught me that a sincere relation, not based on personal interest or agenda, is precious and constitutes a treasure to preserve dearly and enjoy forever. I sincerely hope our friendship will endure and grow stronger with time.

Here, I remember the story of a taxi driver I read one day in a newspaper. It was reported that he once spotted Mr Tata in his car at a traffic light, driving himself, coming from the opposite direction. He waved, then smiled in his direction and Mr Tata returned the courtesy on both occasions. This made him so happy for the rest of the day. When his shift was over, his boss was intrigued to know why his employee was all smiles. The taxi driver told him about his encounter with Mr Tata. 'What did you find unusual or strange in Mr Tata's reaction?' his boss had enquired. The taxi driver commented on his boss's inquiry by saying, 'Sir, money brings you fame, but modesty brings you respect.' What more can I say?!

For all that Mr Tata represents to all Indians and to me, in particular, I decided to single out this personality and dedicate a full chapter, in this book, as a modest attempt to pay a tribute to this living legend, personally, and to those who make of our world a better place, by giving hope and positivity to people around them and to many more, beyond their lands… It is remarkable to meet a person of the stature of Mr Tata, whom I feel has become more important than a head of state, owing to his contribution to the welfare of society and to his legendary modesty. I could never thank him enough for his friendship, and for the love he has shown me and my family, and later on, to my country, which he visited again during the lockdown, along with the Chairman of Tata Sons, Mr Natarajan Chandrashekaran. They spent a full week in Morocco, mainly in Tangiers, in the middle of lockdowns everywhere. I can't express how deeply privileged and honoured we felt to know that the first destination they both decided to visit, when the pandemic had hardly started to reduce in intensity, was to my country… a big honour that says it all.

I still keep my promise and I try as much as I can to meet him, spend quality time in his company, whenever I am visiting Mumbai and his agenda permits, if he is in town. The value of friendship is priceless, and at the end of the day, we are in need of genuine friends. I am extremely humbled when he tells me that I am a "true friend" of his. I pray to the Almighty to bestow on him the best of health and to give him a long life to continue inspiring people, reminding us that solidarity and sharing with others are more important than accumulating wealth. How it is used makes all the difference. God bless him and his ilk, who serve their community altruistically. The world is in need of these kinds of people now more than ever.

Chapter 18

What Doesn't... Makes You Stronger

I have certainly mentioned earlier that there are a few events which occurred in my life that are independent of my own will, or that of my close family, but have impacted me tremendously and shaped my life to the extent of changing the angle of my thinking towards a very philosophical perception of life itself. The first, as you could guess, was the Cameroon burglary, and then there is this most serious one, which I invite you to unveil through the reading of this chapter.

The event dates back to early March 2006, when the then President of the United States of America, George W. Bush, was scheduled to pay an official visit of a few days to Islamabad, Pakistan, where I had been posted as Deputy Head of Mission since September 2003.

I knew beforehand that the security would be drastic and naturally very tight throughout and around the capital. The movement would therefore be restricted, and there would be many checkpoints. Potential threats of terror attacks were also serious and very plausible, mainly because of the American policy, involvement in the war, and in the politics of the neighbouring country, Afghanistan. So, I decided to travel with my family to the farthest city in Pakistan, without leaving the country. Otherwise, I would have to request for leave permission from my Ministry. Karachi was the ideal city candidate for my plan. I called my travel agent, the owner of Omar Travels, Mr Omar Durrani, and requested him to arrange my flight bookings, as well as my stay, at the Marriott Hotel where the General Manager was a good friend of mine, who would be happy to facilitate our stay and also make us feel at home.

In hardly two hours' time, everything was arranged. Our flight was initially scheduled for 9 o'clock in two days' time, on a Thursday, because there were no available seats on the afternoon flights the previous day. However, my friend Omar called the next day to inform me that three seats had been cancelled and become available in the afternoon flight on Wednesday, knowing that it would be more comfortable to spend the night in Karachi, and then enjoy and benefit from being there for the whole day. We therefore booked those seats, and the flight was only four hours from the time we had been informed about the new schedule. We hardly had time to arrange our luggage properly and take all that we would need.

On arrival at the airport, check-in was completed and there were no available seats combined together in a single row. During my yearly holidays, in my different postings, we used to always upgrade our tickets to business class to enjoy more legroom, greater luggage allowance, and more comfort. However, during our travels for tourism, we did not, nor could we afford to follow this custom, for budgetary reasons. It so happened that on board this flight, my wife and daughter's seats were next to a man who visibly had recently undergone surgery and was bandaged all around, while mine was a few rows behind. Our barely nine-year-old child was visibly scared, the prospect of the discomfort overwhelmed her, while keeping her eyes all the time in my direction, as if imploring me to do something and save her from that "unbearable" situation on board. Then she told me, in a barely audible voice, 'Papa, wasn't there any available seats in the business class?'

Even though I couldn't hide the fact that I was also stressed and uncomfortable due to the overall flight conditions, I was more furious with her, on account of what she had just uttered. In the middle of all this, I ordered her to take a pen and paper, or a tissue, or whatever she could write on, and note down what I was going to dictate to her. 'Taking a flight is already a privilege that billions of people cannot afford. And taking it from whatever class is already an extravagance for many.' But deep within myself I knew that the conditions of the two classes are not the same and the difference in comfort is huge. I added that 'The plane is only a means to go from place "A" to "B" and is not an end in itself. Besides, all passengers will arrive at the same time.' She was made to write all this on a tissue, the only thing available in that hurry and mess. I asked her to keep this tissue with her for the rest of her life.

I don't know if she has kept that tissue since then, but I'm sure that she kept it for a long time and, most importantly, understood well and got the lesson right.

Fortunately, the flight was not long and we reached our destination on time. Once in Karachi, everything went smoothly until we reached our hotel. We didn't have to hire a taxi, as the hotel provided us with the transport. For a fun trip, our first evening was pleasant but quiet, even too quiet for me, except for a few minutes of chatting with the General Manager, my good friend Farooq, who was very kind and made sure we had a comfortable and enjoyable stay in his hotel in Karachi. The night view from the eighth floor of our room, at the Marriott Hotel, revealed the expanse and the hugeness of the economic capital of Pakistan. However, from within, you don't see the huge crowds, nor can you hear the noisy environment, or feel the pollution that such a big city naturally can have.

Karima and Ghita were early sleepers and early risers—exactly the opposite of my preference during travels and weekends. So in the "early" morning hours the heavy curtains were widely opened and their voices were audible and intentionally loud to wake me up and disturb my peaceful sleep, arguing that we were on holiday and needed to use time to profit fully from our stay, instead of succumbing to laziness and unhealthy sleep—or so they would keep arguing.

After having succeeded in pulling me from my bed at eight in the morning, the debate started on the programme of the day and how it should be utilised, mainly from where to start. My daughter Ghita and I were of the view that we go for a good swim before breakfast, while Karima had a different view. She was arguing that she had got up quite early and she needed to have breakfast, at the earliest, but in our company.

When we couldn't come to a consensus, I requested them to give me some time to do my morning prayers, after which I would abide by whatever they had decided. I promised not to argue any longer. While positioning myself towards the *Qibla*, in the direction of Mecca, which was incidentally right in front of the window and as I was laying the prayer mat, I found that the morning sun rays were filling all the room and the light was literally dazzling. So, I went almost mechanically to the curtain and drew it nearly completely, leaving hardly 30 cm of opening for the light to filter in, in order to avoid turning on the electric light in the daytime. On completion of my prayers, my daughter was still watching cartoons on TV with her shorts on, without being ready yet to accept the preference of her mother. The temptation to swim was too high, and the blueness of the swimming pool and its crystal clear water looked, from that height, very tantalising. However, we agreed to start by having breakfast and then go for a swim.

While I was in the corridor of the room, taking my shoes from the rack, there was a deafening sound, followed by a violent shaking across the whole hotel. It felt like strong waves after a tsunami, filling the room with sound and airwaves, instead of water. Its force was so strong that it broke the double lock of the door, pulling it off completely, and fortunately, only one side of the door. Sounds of shattering glass from all the windows of the hotel were making a splashing and almost an endless noise, while falling into the pool and on the ground surrounding it, while the bigger part of that crushed glass fell into the swimming pool. This part, which I discovered shockingly later on, I could not share with either of them, at least at that time.

My shirt, which I remember well even now, had stripes of grey and dark lines. It was literally cut from the back and torn in a diagonal manner from top to down, by a sharp piece of glass, which ended up piercing into the other room's door, showing the strength and power of the movement of the glass of not less than eight millimetres width. In that fraction of a second we didn't know what had happened, but I saw my wife running to my daughter who was screaming, only to discover that a few pieces of that thick glass were encrusted in my daughter's legs, the right one mainly, because it was on the side of the window. The TV screen was also broken, either by the sound effect or by the glass window. As you can imagine, the power went off immediately in all the building as the main electric board exploded.

While still in shock and not fully realising what had happened, an even more powerful explosion followed. This one was deafening enough to give the impression that our room was targeted directly by a missile because of the fury of the sound and the flashing light of the fire in the room. With the double explosions, we could barely hear one another, and a very deep voice in the corridors began requesting the guests to leave their rooms immediately by the exit stairs. The trembling voice also said that it was a terrorist attack on the adjacent road.

As you can imagine, since the electricity went off, all the money, the credit card, and the travel documents were still in the safe box, which couldn't be opened. But we had to leave because at that time we didn't know if it was the hotel which was targeted, as the fear of an armed attack by terrorists was present naturally in our minds, since it was frequent at that time. *Madame* took a big white towel and wiped off the bleeding legs of my daughter, and then we headed, altogether, towards the emergency stairs of the hotel. We had to go down eight floors into the "unknown".

While we were moving rapidly, we noticed that every floor was littered with broken glass, making it even more difficult to make our way through. All our focus at that time—if any focus remained, to be honest—was on how to get emergency care very soon for our daughter. At that instant, and while we were hurrying through the debris, with big steps, I don't remember, even now, whether we were capable of keeping our common sense. After a few minutes, which seemed like eternity, we found ourselves amongst the big crowd downstairs, outside in the hotel car parking area, with a good number of ambulances and police forces, coming from everywhere. An officer, who guessed that we were foreigners, feeling lost and not knowing what to do, but visibly looking for urgent assistance, guided us towards one of the ambulances, instructing the driver to head swiftly to a public hospital emergency department, known for receiving the injured in such circumstances and where we could find doctors and necessary first aid equipment.

The ambulance was a Suzuki car, like a matchbox. So when it was moving fast, it became a more serious threat as the risk of an accident was increasing mile after mile. At that moment, I found myself shouting at the driver for his careless driving and for putting our lives in danger. We were all scared, caring more at that time about our overall safety rather than about our daughter's bleeding.

On our way to the hospital, I called a friend, Doctor Behroz Hashim, an ophthalmologist, the son of our former Honorary Consul in Karachi. He joined us immediately after we reached the hospital, while the doctors stitched my daughter's wounds. It was, of course, a great relief to see him there because, apart from being a family friend and a doctor, he was a great help in communication with the staff. But as one can imagine, since there were many people with more serious injuries, the first aid for my daughter was done in haste, given her minor injuries in comparison with the others. Under these circumstances, I think it was quite natural that the emergency staff were concentrating more on saving lives than being meticulous about performing a neat or aesthetic procedure.

What struck me in the successive events is the strength of *Madame* at that moment, making things easier for me. But above all, it was the courage that my daughter had shown which brought great relief and surprise to all of us, including the doctors and the medical staff. She was exchanging pleasantries with them while being stitched, without anaesthesia, saying, 'Don't worry, it will go quickly. I feel fine.' In fact, in hindsight, she was giving to all of us all courage and, to the others, optimism.

After the first aid was completed, my friend Dr Behroz was insisting on taking us home while the hotel was offering us accommodation in another hotel of the same standard. We decided to totally dismiss the idea of lodging again in a hotel in Karachi at that time, for fear of another terrorist attack. Besides, it was easier to do the after-treatment and observation at home. After dropping off my wife and daughter at the house he was sharing with his mother, he drove me back to the hotel where we discovered the scale of that terrorist attack, which had targeted the Vice Consul of the Consulate of the United States, in Karachi. The terrorists, being unable to move into action in Islamabad because of the tight security measures during the visit of George W. Bush, had decided to make themselves heard by perpetrating a terrorist attack against an American official, who unfortunately lost his life along with his driver and two bodyguards, in the bombing of his car.

The Marriott hotel being at a very short walking distance from the Consulate of the USA, a loaded car with bombs, ready to be activated from a distance, was arranged and parked on the road, which the targeted person used to take regularly. We also discovered that the second blast happened as a consequence of the first one, as a CNG car, which was parked nearby, caught fire and then its cylinder exploded. Right after the incident, I kept asking myself what those perished people had done to deserve such a way to be "extinguished", without forgetting the many others who were injured, because of their cowardly act.

The lesson I learnt from all these events is that we always return to our destined path. The attack happened exactly at the time I was meant to be on the plane that day, but fate placed me elsewhere; I was to be present in the blast. Everything was arranged so that we would be there. Needless to say that when such an event happens to anyone, especially if the person survives, they become more mature and certainly go on with a different perception of life. You, then, understand that life and death coexist in every second of our life, but we are certainly shaken out of our comfort zone where we believe that it only happens to the others, while we are the "others" for the rest.

The next day of the event, all newspapers published the photo of Karima holding Ghita in her arms. I remember that the correspondent of Al-Jazeera Channel had called me to enquire about the identity of the "Moroccan lady", reported by the media, who may have been injured in the bomb blast. I told him, 'The lady you are talking about is my daughter, and I want to obstruct anything that could alert my family in Morocco.' I was asking this out of friendship from him. He was very much disappointed to be prevented from an excellent scoop that would have given him a good story of the day. "The Deputy Ambassador of Morocco and his family were caught in the bomb blast, and his daughter was injured in the terrorist attack." That was one of the titles used by the local papers in Karachi while my friend was "dying" to reproduce the same story live on his worldwide channel. I thanked him sincerely for keeping his promise and respecting my privacy.

I have said earlier that we all move towards our destiny. We may have the impression, at times, that we have certain control over our lives and even make attempts to change the path predestined for us. The fact is that we don't and we cannot, as I am fully convinced that everything happens in its own time, in its due course, with a reason and for a purpose that we are unable to perceive, until it is disclosed to us.

In my remembrance of the events, especially those from which I emerged stronger, I would never be able to measure the blessings and the generosity of the Almighty for being still alive and even to be sharing these instances with you. So, I can't deny that the journey itself from those moments until now has been healing in a manner that brings the comfort of closure and an assured sense of clarity. That's why I have always considered that the things which have come, unselectively, back to me are simply true, and raw in their nature. Somehow, it has also been an inner quest, which in itself has been gratifying.

In fact, as I mentioned much earlier, I believe that the indisputable truth that affects us all, in the same manner, is simply *death*, towards which we are getting closer day after day. In reality, we want to forget that the countdown starts from our birth. However lengthy our lives may be, the time we are given on Earth is never enough, and we strive towards living longer. Throughout history, the love of living longer has not been paralleled by anything else. Eternity has been the dream, or rather the mirage, both the kings and paupers have a hankering for.

However, our souls and the time allotted to us on Earth are, fortunately, in God's hands. Our time is indeed insignificant compared to the *infinity* of the universe. Hence, while we are collectively moving towards a particular end, and destiny, the most important thing to be mindful of, I've always believed, is still to live a little more joyfully; even more importantly to give meaning to our lives and try, as much as we can, to make people around us happy and especially those dear to us.

Chapter 19

We Have Come Thus Far

At the outset, I would like to put on record that this chapter, dealing with India-Morocco relations, has been a truly difficult one to write. To be honest, I have resisted the pressing requests from friends and a few editors, as well, to do it in whatever form I want. They knew beforehand that to engage in such an endeavour goes beyond my own logic and nature, driven by built-in and factual motivations. They insisted and have argued that without a chapter on India-Morocco relations, no matter how small it may be, the book would not be complete, and the readers would be left with a feeling of an unaccomplished expectation. Yet, their valid argument didn't diminish the fact that it is a difficult task, as I have always preferred to concentrate on the actions ahead rather than on the ones already done and that are already part of the past. I also argued that there are other ways to make these actions known, either through social media or a publication in our magazine *Morocco in Focus*, issued yearly on the occasion of the celebrations of the Enthronement Day, on the 30th of July. To put it differently, my education, certainly influenced by my beliefs, whereby my left hand should not know what my right hand gives, has a lot to do with this. However, my difficulty in writing the chapter is not limited to what has been said earlier, but stems from much more complex reasons.

First, my tenure is still in progress in this friendly country and, as such, I should observe by obligation a certain reservation from writing about my work. The second reason is linked to the first because, despite the fact that the proposal to write such a chapter is still valid and, to some extent, a good suggestion, it doesn't come without a set of complexities, as it evokes the issues of *why* and *what* I should write. Thirdly, I have always felt uncomfortable when it comes to speaking about myself and the actions to be or already undertaken, be they within the guidelines and instructions of my higher chain of command, or at my initiative or, at the suggestion of any of my colleagues, but in which I am involved and completely responsible for. However, since I have accepted to pen down this chapter, let's follow the *diktat* of *first things first*.

When I was appointed as the Ambassador of His Majesty the King of Morocco to this great and important country, with a rich tradition and heritage, I was, as you can imagine, deeply honoured, extremely happy, and proud to say the least. With its demographic size, the level of its technological advancements and the contribution of its large diversified people, as well as its diaspora, towards its dynamism and development, India is and will remain, a big player both regionally and internationally; a country which contributes to maintaining peace and security and influences global politics and economy. It is also, and above all, a country with which Morocco, being one of the oldest nation states in the world with a great civilisation as well, shares values and, to a certain extent, a common heritage.

Therefore, when the fever of excitement, linked to my appointment in this high function, was digested, the happiness and personal pride were soon hindered by a set of questions and apprehensions with regard to the immensity and complexity of the job. Fortunately, since I had been the Head of Asia and Oceania Directorate at the Ministry of Foreign Affairs and Cooperation for a good number of years, I had had the privilege of visiting many Asian countries, including India. Hence, I knew what lay ahead, where our bilateral relations stood and what was to be or should be done, according to the assessment done, especially with a partner gaining importance year after year, like India. Indeed, the country of Mahatma Gandhi has occupied an important position, which is in line with the new orientations of our foreign policy, especially with regard to the decision of His Majesty Mohammed VI to diversify Morocco's international partners.

On a general note, I find it relevant, beforehand, to point out our people-to-people connection. India has always had a positive perception, not only for me but also for most Moroccans. I remember that when somebody had a hot temper or became nervous, we would advise him to be like Indians: to be calm, zen-like, and mainly tolerant. We also have many people addicted to Indian movies, to the extent that there are many movie theatres or cinemas which have screened exclusively Indian movies every day since the early sixties of the previous century. The result is that many of these "unconditional lovers" speak, or at least understand, Hindi. They have learned it through songs while watching these movies regularly and without having touched the soil of India, or gone to school to learn this language, spoken by people living thousands of miles away. Needless to say, these people knew most of the songs from the movies by heart, as they would listen to them, almost endlessly.

As for the admirers of India from the younger generation, they are more organised and a few of them have studied Hindi at university and are constituted into associations, in different parts of Morocco. They organise many activities, mainly, and not limited to, the celebration of the International Yoga Day. I consider them true ambassadors of India in Morocco. Last, but not least, and as a manifestation of this strong link, Morocco celebrated, in December 2012, during the 9th edition of the Marrakech Film Festival, before India itself, One Hundred Years of Indian Cinema. The objective was to pay tribute to the legends, actors and people who were behind the flourishing of this important entertainment industry, who have brought happiness for decades to hundreds of millions around the world, including people in my country. His Majesty the King decorated many well-known actors on this occasion, mainly Amitabh Bachchan and Shah Rukh Khan. I thought it important to mention these particular things which have connected the two peoples for a long time, and to underline that India is one of the most well-known and liked countries for the Moroccan common man. Even for my mother, who has little knowledge of foreign countries or broad geographical understanding, I didn't have much to explain to her about where I was posted, as she already knew India. So, somehow, my appointment as Ambassador to India was generally welcomed by family, friends, and colleagues.

Furthermore, I was also lucky, in the sense that my posting to New Delhi came hardly one year after the historic meeting between His Majesty King Mohamed VI and the Honourable Prime Minister, Narendra Modi, which took place in Delhi during the month of October 2015, on the margins of the Third India-Africa Summit. It was in that meeting that the two leaders decided to elevate the relations between the two countries into a strategic partnership. It was held a while after Morocco had started to make a big shift in its foreign policy by diversifying its partners. It consisted of building stronger partnerships with new emerging powers and economies, without necessarily affecting or weakening the long-standing and already existing ones with its traditional partners. Naturally, India, among a few others, emerged as one of these countries with which Morocco, already had good relations, but should build stronger and strategic relations.

So, needless to say, as you may have guessed, the burden that I had started to feel, even before starting my work in New Delhi, after the two leaders had instructed their respective governments to build the content and the necessary framework to make this strategic partnership a reality, instead of keeping this decision on paper only. Therefore, work and preparations with different stakeholders had started before travelling to India. I had in mind, somehow, a sort of road map to implement. So, I should believe that the Indian Envoy to Morocco must have felt the same thing. Nevertheless, while admitting that the target was clear in my mind, I had no clear picture of how to go about it, as it was a completely new environment. Besides, a deeper understanding of the country and its people, politically, socially, and above all culturally, was needed before I could embark seriously on this journey.

I also knew, to a large extent, that while in India, my colleagues and I, both Indians and Moroccans, should put in the necessary efforts to reach this objective. It was for us, various stakeholders, to move these relations from a normal and traditional one to a strategic one. For that, we needed to transform our relations from a bilateral trade exchange, in which the larger part was covered by fertilisers and phosphate, to a broader relationship that would be mutually and equally beneficial, covering many more sectors, including those that could be qualified as "sensitive" and "strategic". I was also convinced that there are certain heights that could not be reached without first appointing a Defence Attaché and, second, reinforcing and updating the existing legal framework. This would facilitate for the two governments to prepare concrete content and to set up the necessary mechanisms.

Therefore, when I reached New Delhi I started, as should any newly appointed diplomat, to to meet people, my fellow Ambassadors and officials mainly at the level of the Ministry of External Affairs of this country, which I had known only as a visitor, and now I should discover as a resident diplomat. So, very often, while meeting people, either for courtesy calls, with officials or others, especially for the first time, there would be a set of repetitive questions, somehow, to break the ice. These could be divided mainly into two or three prominent ones. The first one was naturally, but surprisingly as well, about how I found India. The question itself was intriguing because India could not be subsumed in a few lines; it needs books and books. After a while, I somehow got accustomed to this question, since it was to start conversations and much more, a rhetorical one, rather than a request for information.

Even after a few years serving in India, I still find it difficult to answer this particular question easily, not because I haven't done my homework, but mainly because the country is a dynamic society, changing very quickly and cannot be fully understood through a single angle. It is a very diverse country, with 28 states and 8 union territories, where each one is different from the others in many ways, including, at times, language, culture, and food, yet united. Furthermore, since many important things and events do not always happen and exclusively in Delhi, a diplomat has to travel extensively, to its various states and regions to understand the different facets, similarities and contradictions, but, more importantly, the hidden treasures and beauty of this fascinating country-continent.

Hence, the diversity in India needs to be seen more as a source of richness of the country. This is true mainly because, I believe, people in different parts of India have not been static. Those from the south, the north, the west or the east have been, throughout history, in constant movement looking for a better life, opportunities or jobs, for good education or for security reasons. Each part has influenced and been influenced by the other, the result being a united nation of different, yet close customs, with nuances from one region to the other. With its rich culture, there are in India endless kinds of folk music, of dances, of handicrafts and architecture, making a unique mixture between different layers of people, cultures, religions and ethnicities, a fascinating mixture making the country a mosaic tableau that changes constantly as you travel from north to south or east to west.

The second question would naturally be related to the status of the relations between Morocco and India, and here I find myself obliged to draw two distinctions. The first relates to how far back we are connected, our commonly known history, because there is always an unknown side of history which remains veiled, to our regret. Here, I don't need to go extensively into speaking about the Moroccan travellers since the 11th Century, and some of whom were mentioned by the well-known traveller Ibn Batuta through his famous book, the "Rihla" (The Travels), during his travels to and within this country. I am pretty sure that many more Moroccans travelled to this region a few centuries ago. One of the illustrations of our early connection was trade. Through the density of historical references, I wouldn't be surprised if one of the early spice roads linked Kerala to Marrakech as early as the 11th or 12th century.

Then, I would like to veer to the early 20th century, when the last ruler of Kapurthala in Punjab, Maharaja Jagatjit Singh, came back from a visit to Morocco and was left fascinated by the architecture of the big mosque in Marrakesh, the "Koutoubia", a replica of which is also found in Cordoba, Spain. He then decided to build a mosque in 1927 for his Muslim community. This architectural masterpiece was completed in 1930. It became a place of worship for Muslims and an edifice of prime tourist and cultural attraction while visiting Punjab. The Moorish Mosque, its name referring to the people of North Africa, mainly Moroccan, is believed to be one of the most fascinating mosques architecturally in South Asia, according to many surveys. Since its pattern is made along similar lines and almost identical architecture, one feels, at first glance, "deported" to Marrakech. So much is the striking resemblance between the two mosques. But what I like most in this mosque is that, for many historians, it is not only an edifice for worship but also a project which was meant, by this wise and well-educated King, 'To reinforce cohesion and to promote social integration among his people of different confessions', in Punjab. This architectural jewellery represents, for me and for many Indians, a source of shared pride, a strong connection and one of the many links that have happily existed for long between these two old nations.

What I would call the second phase of our relations started, naturally, after the independence era, during which India played a significant role in the decolonisation of many Asian, Latin-American, and African countries, especially within the Non-Aligned Movement, where there has been a good collaboration between our two countries. However, formal diplomatic relations between India and Morocco were established in 1957, less than one year after the independence of the Kingdom of Morocco from the French protectorate. Though their bilateral relations were cordial and imprinted with mutual respect, they didn't witness a strong boost because they were still influenced, even regulated somehow, by the Cold War, East and West alliances, formed after the end of the Second World War.

After their independence, India became much more inclined towards the Eastern side, led by the then Soviet Union, in opposition to Morocco, which was considered to be closer to the Western side, led by the United States. This ideological difference didn't prevent Morocco from having good relations with the "Eastern Camp", including India, with which it enjoyed cordiality, based on the respect for each other's choices. However, these relations had a serious setback when India decided to recognise in 1985, soon after the death of Indira Gandhi, a separatist movement, the "Polisario Front" created initially and financed by Colonel Muammar Gaddafi of Libya. The movement was then adopted by Algeria, which has sheltered its members in its territories since then. Later on, the leaders of this separatist movement proclaimed, on one side, the creation of an entity, so-called the "sahrawi Arab democratic republic", at the instigation of Algeria and with its support financially and diplomatically, in collaboration with Libya and a few other countries, mainly from the Southern African region.

From that time until 1999, the bilateral relations were almost at a halt, even though the Embassy of the Kingdom remained open with a lower-level of representation in New Delhi. This was in itself an exception granted to India, since Morocco was used to closing, in most cases, its Embassy wherever a mission of the separatist movement of Polisario was opened, as a protest against the hostile gesture from the host country. This gesture was widely seen as one of goodwill from the Moroccan side.

The visit of the late Prime Minister of India, Atal Bihari Vajpayee, in 1999 to Morocco marked a turning point in the bilateral relations. Soon after this visit, India withdrew its recognition of this entity and its representation was closed. There followed the appointment of an Ambassador to India in 2000, and the then Prime Minister, late

Abderrahmane Youssoufi, undertook an official visit to Delhi that same year. This new dynamism in the bilateral relations culminated in the first official visit of His Majesty to India as King in 2001. It was the first Asian country he visited after his enthronement, on 30th July 1999.

This visit laid the foundations for a new era of collaboration between the two countries. It paved the way for strategic cooperation in vital sectors, particularly in the domain of agriculture. Morocco's investment in India's agricultural sector, specifically in phosphates and fertilisers, has not only strengthened economic ties but also contributed to India's food security. That is why this visit constituted a strong milestone in the history of our bilateral relations, because it witnessed a major decision from His Majesty to help India achieve and ensure its independence in food security. This decision was highly appreciated by the Indian authorities, since it was based on a political decision, rather than driven by commercial reasons.

I personally believe that each official visit of His Majesty to India constituted a turning point, in that it gave a real impetus to our bilateral cooperation. The second Royal Visit, which took place in the year 2015, further put the bilateral relations in a strategic trajectory and allowed building of a stronger partnership. His Majesty's meeting with Prime Minister Modi proved pivotal in setting the stage for broader cooperation and in establishing the necessary framework for robust and strategic relations.

Despite the growing number of events and keeping in mind the positive evolution of our relations, my difficulties would start again whenever the question of the status of our bilateral relations is raised by somebody. I somehow get the feeling that I am being judged by my interlocutor. However, since it remains a normal query, I find myself trapped and can't dismiss it altogether. If the question is a simple one at first appearance, it also hinders the bigger question of what has been done since my arrival in India. Therefore, it soon becomes a source of self-examination and accountability, and even more a catalyst in pushing me and my colleagues to take action permanently and to work harder in order to further develop our bilateral cooperation in various sectors.

I realised, after a while, that the best way was to divert the dialogue on the subject and to focus on human relations. In this regard, I am truly thrilled to witness the number of friendships that have been developed and the level of trust that the two countries have achieved at different levels, not only as and with officials but also between the business communities and the peoples of both nations, in general.

While doing my personal evaluation about my ongoing stay in the land of Gandhi, it is also important to highlight that, though it is a friendly country, India is not an easy environment to understand, cover or cope with all at once. Indeed, for foreigners, and diplomats in particular, Delhi with its difficult and extreme weather between the rainy, humid seasons, and the dry ones, especially when the heat is coupled with humidity, aggravated by the climate change and deregulation, the density of its population and the severe and hazardous pollution, make the place a challenging milieu and a difficult environment for families.

However, on the other hand, there is no doubt that the kindness of its people, the diversity and the economy of the country provide great opportunities for business and investment, especially outside the capital Delhi. Each state has, indeed, something different to offer, which needs to be unveiled. So, however much effort is put in, we end up having the impression that many things are missed, or yet to be done. This gives me, very often, a sentiment of "non-satisfaction". Thus, as a diplomat, to serve in India is certainly a great and rewarding experience, but it would be pretentious to say that I am content with what has been achieved so far. This feeling of "dissatisfaction" constitutes, at least for me, a kind of driving force to do more, given the fact that it is a fast-growing economy with endless opportunities and possibilities. Therefore, after a while, one realises that the biggest challenge in India is India itself, as it should be seen not as a single country but rather like a whole continent embracing many countries, to be approached separately.

That said, and while doing the difficult exercise of reviewing our bilateral relations and taking stock of the level they have reached, it would be unfair to speak only of myself or my current colleagues, without paying a significant tribute to my predecessors and former colleagues who contributed greatly in building these relations brick by brick until they have reached their current level. On the other hand, it is important to underline that the personal involvement in doing the job with the help of friends, partners and Ministers, makes a great difference in terms of results and promptness of actions. I came to understand, after more than three decades serving as a diplomat, that building credible and genuine friendships is, by all means, what makes a difference between diplomats.

The multiple connections and personal relations do help, undoubtedly, in implementing quite a good number of actions that would not have been possible without the personal involvement of Ministers in the governments of both countries, with whom I have taken it as an obligation to know personally, and to maintain my relationships with them continuously. Regardless of the assistance they may provide when in need, I strongly believe that knowing people is in itself a treasure that never depletes.

One of the things I have been proud of doing, so far, is that during my yearly holiday in Morocco, I would dedicate a few days of my own vacation to pay courtesy calls to different Ministers of my Government in Rabat, mainly those who manage sectors to be closely developed with India, or whose portfolios represent a particular interest for both countries. I believe that when people recognise in you the genuine personal involvement in pushing things to happen, and when you establish personal links with members of the government, from both sides, you definitely shorten the distance, in making things move faster and more efficiently. The connections certainly help in avoiding the unnecessary heaviness of the administrative procedure, at times. The result is that Ministers give a little bit more importance and effort to fostering the relations because they become personally involved in putting a bit of their own into the bigger target set by the leaders.

However, I should confess that at the beginning, it was a challenge to mobilise Ministers, from both sides, to travel this long distance in order to nurture bilateral visits or participate in international events. But soon after the interest was created about the importance of the two countries in their respective regions, a fluidity of high-level visits started to take place, generating more and more significance.

It is also important to underline that since India has always been a good partner of Morocco, with a strong mutual support, in different forums and international organisations, the Embassy didn't have much difficulty in establishing strong relations with the officials at the Ministry of External Affairs. Indeed, the personal and close relations with the Indian officials have always been a great asset and have proven to be of great assistance in achieving the objectives and in facilitating different actions to be implemented. As we have been aware of the importance of the tasks assigned to all of us, it was in our mutual interest to cooperate closely at different levels.

After a few years spent in this position, I have come to believe strongly that good relations between nations, especially on the political level, based on mutual respect and understanding, are essential not only in implementing actions towards building strategic relations but for the bilateral ties to always grow further. But, to make them sustainable and everlasting, they need other essential elements relating to developing economic and people-to-people relations.

For these reasons, I believe that after a few years, the strong relations, which I can confidently qualify as strategic, between Morocco and India does stand on four pillars which constitute the backbone of their bilateral relations. These axes needed to be corroborated by not only updating the existing legal framework but also by reinforcing it to meet the ambitions of both countries. The first pillar would be the enhancement of economic ties through more diversified trade and investment, facilitating sustainable growth and development between the two nations. This would not be efficient without involving more exchanges on the level of the two business communities and facilitating their integration in both economies.

The second pillar would reinforce bilateral cooperation in sensitive sectors, which include defence, security to promote regional stability, and to address common threats. Here, it is important to mention that the appointment in 2022, by Morocco of a Defence Attaché, which constituted a strong signal and an important element of the action plan of the Embassy, reflected the ambition of the Highest Authorities of my country to cooperate with India in this important and strategic sectors, by opening new possibilities and reaching new heights in their strategic relations.

Thirdly, cultural and people-to-people exchanges are essential in cementing this partnership, whose objective is to deepen the mutual understanding and encourage the easy flow of their citizens to their respective countries. Hence, the inclusion of Indians among the first beneficiaries of the services of the e-visa to enter Morocco, without prior conditions, opened widely the door for Indians to visit Morocco, whose number is growing steadily month after month.

The fourth pillar remains of paramount importance as it focuses on addressing jointly the global challenges, including climate change, cybersecurity, and combatting terrorism, to name but a few, through collective and concerted action. The collaboration between the two countries in these areas is effective, sound and growing on a win-win basis.

Our collective efforts to give concrete content to the relations that the two nations have aspired to make strategic have allowed to materialise more than thirty ministerial-level visits from both sides in the span of few years, with a slight numerical edge from the Moroccan side. Of course, the high rhythm of visits was forced to slow down because of the COVID pandemic. Indeed, for more than two years, there were almost no movements on either side, like elsewhere around the world. However, the generosity shown by India during the pandemic, by providing a substantial number of vaccines on a commercial basis (seven million doses), was highly appreciated and valued by all Moroccans. This proved how India had been and would remain a reliable partner on which Morocco could count. The vaccine purchased from India greatly helped the Government of the Kingdom of Morocco to conduct its vaccination campaign successfully, with the help of other partners, at different stages.

On the level of the bilateral legal framework, the two countries have managed to organise two joint bilateral commissions, one in Rabat and the other in Delhi, to build a stronger legal framework comprising around fifty agreements and memoranda of understanding, which have been concluded during the last few years, covering different sectors of cooperation, ranging from health, infrastructure, security, cyber security, space, counter terrorism, vocational training, education, foreign affairs, to economy and trade.

Our bilateral trade benefited also from the positive trend that our relations have witnessed in recent years. Indeed, in the course of this exercise, we moved from USD 1.2 billion during the budget year 2015–2016 to a record high of USD 4.1 billion in 2022-2023, according to the official statistics released by the Moroccan "Office de Change". On the other side, there is a great matter of satisfaction when we observe the steadily growing presence of Indian companies in Morocco. While they numbered thirteen before the visit of His Majesty's in 2015, the current count is around forty-five, with huge prospects of growth in sectors such as IT, Energy, Defence, Health, Pharmaceuticals, Green Hydrogen, Infrastructure, the automotive sector, and so on.

Apart from these elements, I can say with confidence that the remarkable aspect of Morocco-India relations has been the unwavering support that both nations have extended to each other. This support transcends borders and is particularly evident in matters of vital importance, such as the respect for each other's territorial integrity and national sovereignty. These are principles that both countries advocate for constantly on different occasions, and which guide their foreign policy.

In being pushed to overcome the daunting endeavour or even the "ordeal" of speaking of what has been done collectively, I can say that there are enough things we should be proud to have achieved, and equally, there are many other things in which we have not succeeded in materialising. The importance is to spare no effort in fulfilling our duties in the best manner possible, at least to our modest knowledge.

More importantly, from the lessons I have learned, I have come to understand that failures should never make us give up, come what may. Besides, I concluded that diplomats should be patient and perseverant in their endeavours. After a few years spent in Delhi, I would say that we have had a fairly positive journey, my colleagues and I, while working towards reinforcing and contributing to bringing these bonds closer and in making our bilateral relations stronger year after year.

In saying this, I am fully aware that many other elements are to be taken into consideration in achieving these results. At the top of these is, undoubtedly, the strong will from the Highest Authorities in both countries to bring these associations to a level that would reflect, not only the historical and long-standing relations that go back for centuries, but also by taking advantage of the endless opportunities that each country offers to their respective business communities. Both countries are emerging powers in their respective regions, with India becoming a more global one as well. This fact offers both of them endless opportunities to seize, either bilaterally, regionally or globally. It also entails for them more responsibilities to contribute to global security.

I also believe that one of the main achievements remain the evolution of perception of the Indians, especially the business people, about Morocco, as they have started to use my country as an important base for growth and a platform for their exports, not only to Africa and the Arab world, but also to North America and Europe.

The facilities and easy access to these markets, owing to the different Free Trade Agreements that Morocco has with these entities, attract more and more investments from many countries, including India. Of course, the role of the governmental entities, including the Embassy I have the honour to lead, has been mainly to promote, encourage and facilitate the business communities' collaboration, as well as to bring the different institutions closer.

In achieving this, I will always remain indebted to all my Indian colleagues and friends at different levels, especially all the officials at the Ministry of External Affairs and from other Ministries, organisations and institutions I have dealt with and those I haven't had the chance to meet personally. Without their contribution, help and assistance, we would not have achieved what we have and been where we are now. I am confident that the future and perspectives of our cooperation appear more promising.

I would like to take this opportunity to pay a special tribute to my family for their invaluable support, which has been the real driving force in enabling me to reach where I am. A special tribute to my better half and lovely spouse Karima, who has done a tremendous job in her softer side of diplomacy, by being closely involved with the Indian society, and in managing different groups like Delhi Commonwealth Women's Association (DCWA) and the Spouses of Heads of Mission (SHOM), and other regional groups for charity and education. To be honest, and as I have said earlier, one could never measure the importance that spouses of diplomats, men and women, can bring in fostering people-to-people relations and in facilitating better understanding between the countries of origin and those of accreditation. Spouses constitute undoubtedly a real asset in bridging cultures and in reinforcing understanding.

IndiePress

The best route your story can take.

To publish your own book, contact us.

We publish poetry collections, short story collections, novellas and novels.

contact@indie-press

www.ingramcontent.com/pod-product-compliance
Lightning Source LLC
Chambersburg PA
CBHW030334010526
44119CB00028B/395/J